Praise for OUR HIGHER CALLING

"Clearly and appealingly written, this book is an important call for universities to reimagine their partnerships with society. Thorp and Goldstein combine the benefits of their own deep experience with interviews with key educational figures and offer insight on nearly every major issue facing universities today. I enjoyed this book from beginning to end."
—Christopher Newfield, author of *The Great Mistake: How We Wrecked Public Universities and How We Can Fix Them*

"American higher education has long enjoyed intricate partnerships with government and society, but in recent decades, those have frayed. Thorp and Goldstein offer penetrating insights about the challenges faced as well as a comprehensive prescription for a new and enduring compact."
—Mary Sue Coleman, president, Association of American Universities

"For more than a century, a strong system of American higher education has been one of the greatest drivers for prosperity, not just in our own country but in the world. This thought-provoking book shows that our future depends on restoring a common understanding of the purpose of higher education. With a clear-eyed sense of challenges and failings in our colleges and universities, Thorp and Goldstein also show the elements of meaningful strategies to address demographic, technological, and other changes."
—Peter Grauer, chairman, Bloomberg L.P.

"It is high time for fresh thinking and new urgency in how higher education is preparing students for careers after graduation. We must nurture people's curiosity so they have the desire and ability to continuously develop their skills. This book shows how higher education and those seeking to employ college and university graduates can ensure they are pulling in the same direction as we seek a prosperous and productive future."
—Jonas Prising, chairman and CEO, ManpowerGroup

"American higher education faces significant challenges, but they are not insurmountable. In this book, Holden Thorp and Buck Goldstein dispel myths and recommend solutions that must be taken seriously. A degree from an American university is still the envy of the world. The ideas shared in this book show how that can remain true in the future."
—Gururaj "Desh" Deshpande, serial entrepreneur and life member, MIT Corporation

"A growing chorus of voices is insisting that the world's great problems will be solved only through innovative thinking and that such thinking can best be found at the research university. Right at the forefront of this group are Holden Thorp . . . and Buck Goldstein . . . and they lay out a persuasive case in *Engines of Innovation*."
—*BizEd*

"Thorp and Goldstein have hit the mark. Promoting innovation in higher education is one of the best things we can do for our country's global competitiveness and economic future, and this book points the way forward."
—Michael R. Bloomberg, former mayor of New York City

"Universities have enabled the American dream and are among our nation's greatest competitive strengths. However, the costs of a university education are unsustainably high, and there is pressure on virtually every traditional source of revenue. Universities must transform themselves, yet they face numerous barriers to change—starting with the tenure system. This book, by one of the new generation of innovative university presidents together with a leading venture capitalist, describes how universities can embark on a whole new path. The book is full of ideas for university leaders, trustees, alumni, philanthropists, and the business community."
—Michael E. Porter, Harvard Business School

"Thorp and Goldstein bring an urgent and timely message: American universities must fundamentally transform in order to assure America's global competitive leadership in the 21st century. Simply put, if colleges foster an entrepreneurial culture, innovation will flourish, both within our academic institutions and more broadly throughout the economy. This outstanding book paves the way forward."
—John Denniston, partner at Kleiner Perkins Caufield & Byers

"*Engines of Innovation* inspires, guides, and informs universities on collaboration, structure, sustainability, cost, and practical details of designing and achieving maximum potential for entrepreneurship programs. This fascinating read is an excellent resource for helping universities connect with the world beyond their campuses."
—Deborah D. Hoover, president and CEO of the
Burton D. Morgan Foundation

Our Higher Calling

Our Higher Calling

Rebuilding the Partnership between America and Its Colleges and Universities

Holden Thorp and Buck Goldstein

THE UNIVERSITY OF NORTH CAROLINA PRESS Chapel Hill

This book was published with the assistance of the Luther H. Hodges Sr. and Luther H. Hodges Jr. Fund of the University of North Carolina Press.

Designed by Richard Hendel
Set in Utopia
by codeMantra, Inc.
Manufactured in the United States of America

The University of North Carolina Press has been a member of the Green Press Initiative since 2003.

Jacket illustration: *Group of Diverse International Students Celebrating Graduation* by Rawpixel, iStockphoto.com

Library of Congress Cataloging-in-Publication Data
Names: Thorp, H. Holden, 1964– author. | Goldstein, Buck, author.
Title: Our higher calling : rebuilding the partnership between America and its colleges and universities / Holden Thorp and Buck Goldstein.
Description: Chapel Hill : The University of North Carolina Press, [2018] | Includes bibliographical references and index.
Identifiers: LCCN 2018008894| ISBN 9781469646862 (cloth : alk. paper) | ISBN 9781469646879 (ebook)
Subjects: LCSH: Education, Higher—United States—Philosophy. | Education, Higher—Aims and objectives—United States. | Universities and colleges—United States.
Classification: LCC LB2322.2 .T48 2018 | DDC 378.73—dc23
LC record available at https://lccn.loc.gov/2018008894

For John, Emma, Katherine, and Max

Contents

Our Higher Calling

Introduction

When we published our book *Engines of Innovation*, the two of us asserted that universities could have a greater impact on the world's biggest problems by embracing an entrepreneurial mindset. The favorable response both to the book and to the idea that an entrepreneurial mindset has a place within the university was both gratifying and surprising. Although the interest in entrepreneurship among colleges and universities was already sprouting as we were writing our book, by the time it was published, most universities were actually launching some sort of innovation initiative. As we write this introduction, it is hard to find a college or university in this country or abroad that has not enthusiastically embraced the ideas of innovation and entrepreneurship as part of its curriculum and its culture.[1] This interest in making entrepreneurship part of higher education emerged largely in response to the need for new initiatives in an uncertain economy and for universities to prove their relevance in a time of nationwide upheaval.

Our book generated another surprise. Many readers assumed that when we argued that universities could benefit from entrepreneurial thinking, we were suggesting that the university itself should be run like a business. Nothing could be further from the truth. We do believe that many aspects of the university's operations can benefit from the ideas and ways of thinking developed in the business world. We also believe that commercialization of university ideas and inventions can best be done in partnership with the private sector. But we view these partnerships as essential precisely because the university is not and cannot be run like a commercial enterprise.[2]

The most visible evidence of this last statement is the breathtaking collapse of the for-profit higher education industry. The best-known example is the University of Phoenix, a former darling of Wall Street. The school expanded dramatically in its first years, largely through admitting unqualified students—balance sheets were strong, but admissions standards were lax. After a new president introduced stiffer standards for admittance and took the company private, enrollment dropped: it had been 460,000 students in 2010, but by December 2016, it was 175,000.[3] Meanwhile, in 2015, Corinthian Colleges filed for bankruptcy, closing twenty-eight schools and leaving 16,000 without classes.[4] ITT Educational Services followed suit, shuttering the doors of technical colleges and affecting 35,000 students and 8,000 employees. The move came days after the U.S. Department of Education barred the company from enrolling new students who received federal aid.[5] In a further sign of the disconnect between the for-profit mindset and higher education, one of the leading for-profit entities, Kaplan University, determined that its for-profit model did not work and was acquired in 2017 by the nonprofit Purdue University.[6]

The evidence that colleges and universities cannot be run like a business is not limited to the for-profit sector. A well-known example is the debacle at Mount St. Mary's University, the nation's second-oldest Catholic institution of higher learning, located in Emmitsburg, Maryland. Simon Newman was named the university's president in 2015 largely through his reputation as an accomplished financier and manager, having founded or cofounded four businesses and having worked at various times for Bain & Company, JP Capital Partners, and Cornerstone Management Group. In less than a year, he fashioned a plan to corporatize the school with an emphasis on career education, culminating in his criticizing a professor for thinking of incoming students who were unlikely to succeed as "cuddly bunnies" and suggesting that the professor needed to "drown the bunnies . . . [and] put a Glock to their heads" to improve the school's rankings.[7] The statement ignited a firestorm of internal and national criticism and resulted in the firing of numerous dissenting professors and a threat of loss of accreditation. Ultimately, Newman tendered his resignation.

But if universities cannot be run like corporations, how should they confront the challenges facing higher education today? We believe the answer begins with understanding a partnership that was struck as early as 1636 with the founding of Harvard College, codified more explicitly in 1862 with the passage of the Morrill Act, fleshed out in the 1930s and 1940s with the establishment of an enlightened national science policy, and settled by the 1960s. In his book *Toward a More Perfect University*, Jonathan Cole calls this understanding an implicit compact between American colleges and universities and the government.[8] We believe that this compact can best be characterized as a partnership, not only between universities and the government, but between universities and the public at large. This partnership can be described as follows: in exchange for educating a highly competitive workforce and providing leadership in the discovery of new knowledge applicable to matters of public interest, academic communities will be funded and allowed to run as a meritocracy with the freedom to both explore and espouse disparate and unpopular ideas as well as essentially manage their own affairs.[9]

Viewed from a distance and over the long term, American universities have held up their side of the partnership. Our best institutions of higher learning comprise three-quarters of the top twenty universities in the world, and the United States has three times more Nobel Prize winners than the United Kingdom, which ranks second. College graduates on average have twice the lifetime earnings of nongraduates, and for millions of Americans higher education has become a bridge to the middle class. Nevertheless, it is impossible to ignore the strains that have appeared in that partnership. Americans have become skeptical about whether college is worth it. The skepticism is strongest among young people. An NBC News/Wall Street Journal survey indicates that fewer than 40 percent of Americans ages eighteen to thirty-four now believe that college is worth the cost, down from almost 60 percent just four years earlier.[10] This skepticism has surfaced at the same time that public institutions have sustained drastic reductions in public funding generally and federal support for research has been flat for much of the past decade. It is clear from our own experience while we were researching and writing this book that many Americans believe that the partnership is broken.

Our purpose in writing this book is to examine the elements of this critical partnership, unpack the competing narratives, and recommend a path that clearly articulates the obligations of all sides. The effort to rebuild the partnership will necessarily involve a conversation among parties inside and outside of the university, each with distinctly different points of view, but it is critical that we bridge those divides. Because higher education serves as an extraordinary engine of social mobility and a source of knowledge that critically shapes America's economy and national interest, this conversation has the potential to define the future of the country.

Two competing viewpoints dominate the current discussion on how the partnership can best be reconstituted. One model—championed by many faculty and administrators—involves an unapologetic doubling down by the university on its traditional roles of teaching and research, free of influence from the nonacademic world. The narrative that underlies this idea is that the university produces knowledge and an educated citizenry, outcomes that are priceless and timeless, and that the introduction of systematic management techniques and a narrow focus on student success beyond the university is simply the corporatization of a sacred institution. This approach presumes that the resources that support the university, for example, tuition, government subsidy, and contributions from wealthy donors, should be provided with no strings attached. As far as the needs of students are concerned, those who advocate this model believe that a liberal education is a societal good and that preparation for employment after graduation is secondary.

Those who support this approach maintain that, for reasons that are largely political, government is no longer meeting its obligations to fund higher education adequately, thereby making it impossible for colleges and universities to fulfill their traditional role of educating students for useful and productive lives and generating knowledge that contributes to the public good.

The other approach—championed by many politicians, trustees, and alumni—borrows both language and techniques from the private sector and grafts them onto the organizational structure of the university. In this approach, the university has a transactional relationship with its students, who pay tuition in exchange for a good job and a good life; an employer-employee relationship with its faculty, who are paid to teach a prescribed number of students and, in some cases, compete for and secure a certain amount of grant funding; and a corporate relationship with its governing board. Student success in this model is measured by postgraduate employment rates and graduate starting salaries. New knowledge is valued for its potential to generate a profit for the inventor and the institution. The academic health center is viewed as a commercial enterprise, and the care provided there differs little from that offered by a private entity.

Supporters of this viewpoint argue that resistance to accountability has not served the university or the public well. Furthermore, colleges cost way too much, do not prepare students adequately for a career, and spend excessively on administration and amenities. Some go so far as to assert that higher education has become merely a form of political indoctrination at the taxpayer's expense. And there is no denying that this sort of thinking has already resulted in dramatic reductions in public support and funding for higher education.

In reality, most take a position between these two extremes. Nevertheless, as this blunt summary suggests, battle lines are drawn and areas of potential compromise are hard to identify. And yet, the stakes are too high for us not to try to find them. We believe that such a pathway exists and that the starting point for negotiation lies in the partnership codified with the Morrill Act of 1862, in which the federal government provided the resources necessary to found institutions of higher learning in every state and the universities *provided* a public good and *assumed* a public duty. When the partnership works, higher education produces knowledge that is timeless and priceless, as well as habits of mind that prepare students to be independent, productive thinkers and responsible citizens in a democracy. Staff and faculty view their roles not simply as jobs but rather as near-sacred endeavors. Similarly, the loyalty that colleges and universities engender in their alumni is far greater than that produced by a mere business transaction. At the same time, universities earn the opportunity to operate by providing students with a pathway to economic prosperity and producing knowledge in the public interest.

We do not underestimate the difficulty of rebuilding the partnership we suggest. Academics bridle when administrators talk to them of the impact of their research and its usefulness to society, because they find such conversations demeaning. Trustees and alumni do not always accept the importance of shared governance, academic freedom, and, especially, tenure—all of which are at the foundation of American higher education. Reconciling the competing narratives will require interpersonal capital applied to networks inside and outside of the university. This can only happen following a conversation that celebrates the nuances that make American higher education great while acknowledging that it has to change in response to the challenges ahead.

In truth, successful administrators have been attempting to navigate this partnership for some time. Bart Giamatti, who served as president of Yale University (and later as commissioner of Major League Baseball), framed the challenge this way in 1988: "Being president of a university is no way for an adult to make a living," he wrote. "Which is why so few adults actually attempt to do it. It is to hold a mid-nineteenth-century ecclesiastical position on top of a late-twentieth-century corporation."[11]

To rebuild the partnership, misconceptions such as the following must be tackled head on.

A college degree is not worth the cost. By any measure a college degree—even with debt—is "worth it" as long as you finish: those who do not complete their course of study are worse off than those who never try. So completion rate is just as important a metric for judging success in higher education as student debt.

Colleges and universities are flush with resources. Although seventy-five or so elite colleges and universities have large endowments and other income streams that make them more financially secure, most colleges are struggling financially. More than half of existing institutions have an unsustainable business model and will not survive without profound change. Even the elite schools are threatened by public policies aimed at taxing their endowments and cutting off the flow of "full-pay" foreign students so essential to their business model.

College is a residential experience for students between ages eighteen and twenty-two. In fact, 45 percent of college students are aged twenty-two and over, 28 percent have children, 62 percent work full or part time, and 54 percent live off campus.[12] The actual face of American higher education is vastly different from the way it is perceived by the general public.

American colleges and universities are the front door to the middle class. This is no longer the case. American higher education is losing its claim as a facilitator of income mobility. Students from the top quartile of income are eight times more likely to get a degree than those from the bottom quartile.[13]

The system of academic tenure is no way to run an institution. Academic tenure is in fact an economic boon to higher education. The fundamental business model that allows colleges and universities to survive would be undermined without the attractiveness of tenure to its most important members, because the cost savings from tenure at the beginning of academic careers far outweigh the costs at the end of academic careers.

Colleges and universities are not contributing enough to economic growth. The myth of the lone intellectual sitting in an ivory tower has been exploded by the remarkable economic engine that higher education and its related medical centers have become, and the economic influence of colleges and universities will only increase over time.

Colleges with high sticker prices are out of reach for most students. Many colleges with high tuition sticker prices have progressive financial aid programs that often make them cheaper for low-income students to attend than the public universities in their home states or private colleges with lower sticker prices and less financial aid.

Liberal arts degrees will not result in a good job. By any measure, the intellectual discipline and habits of mind at the heart of the liberal arts are exactly what is required to prepare students for the twenty or so different jobs they will have during their careers. The challenge for the liberal arts is that a good liberal education will not by itself translate into a good job on graduation. The reality is more complex, and job readiness must become an integral part of American higher education at every level.

In the chapters that follow, we attempt to dispel these common misconceptions and take up the real challenges facing higher education. In the first three chapters, we lay out the strengths of the diverse set of institutions that constitute American higher education as well as the challenges they face. We also identify the institutional impediments to developing a strategy that attacks these challenges. Next, we discuss the unique roles in academia of students, faculty, and administration, none of which aligns with concepts from the business world such as customers, employees, or management. We then address the areas where universities can most effectively deliver on public expectations in a way that builds trust and a stronger partnership. Last, we frame what we hope will be a national conversation on rebuilding the partnership and suggest specific approaches that we believe will pave the way for this critical dialogue.

Throughout the book, we describe trends that apply to most any institution. Although it may seem that some apply only to elite institutions or to small colleges, we find that the larger trends apply to all. For example, even though well-endowed private schools have more money, they have to spend more to keep up with their competition. Small schools, for their part, still aspire to compete with schools that they see as aspirational peers; this keeps up a financial pressure that is remarkably similar to that felt at schools with more resources.

The university, and indeed everything embodied in the concept of higher learning, is one of civilization's transcendent and permanent ideas. Universities are enduring and impactful. They change the lives of those who learn and teach inside their walls, and they will outlast most other institutions in our society. Students who are admitted to an institution of higher learning join a community of learners; they do not simply contract for a sequence of courses that provides a credential. Alumni wear the colors and sing the school songs for life because their alma mater has become part of their identity. Faculty work for lower compensation because they believe the curation and transmission of knowledge is a priceless and timeless undertaking of great importance. All of the interested parties have a stake in rebuilding the partnership that makes being part of an American university not just a profession or a business transaction but a higher calling.

{ 1

Why American Universities Are the Best in the World

The partnership between America and its colleges and universities has produced a set of institutions that includes fifteen of the top twenty universities in the world.[1] American universities have evolved to become timeless curators of knowledge and culture, relentless producers of new ideas and technologies, and environments where students can best learn the habits of mind that equip them to be citizens in a democracy. These public goods emerged because American universities also embraced their public duty to provide useful knowledge and talent. This partnership with the public produced a set of fundamental characteristics that combine to make American higher education preeminent, and they must be central to the conversation as the partnership is rebuilt.

THE CURRICULUM IS ANCHORED IN THE LIBERAL ARTS

Although the United States did not invent liberal arts education, the study of science, language, and culture has become an indispensable part of American higher education. Despite a decline in liberal arts enrollments over the past few decades, the college of arts and sciences remains a dominant feature of great universities.[2] Even undergraduate professional schools ground their curricula in the liberal arts tradition, both through the required courses but also—and perhaps more important—through the colocation of professional education in the liberal arts environment. For instance, the criminology and criminal justice major at Eastern Michigan University requires a full set of general education courses, plus classes in philosophy, sociology, and psychology.[3]

American college education continues to focus on the fundamentals of the liberal arts: mastering science as described by Darwin, Newton, and Einstein; reading and analyzing texts by Martin Luther King, Shakespeare, and Chaucer; studying the history of the Western and non-Western worlds; and building an appreciation for art, music, and theater. And while it is popular to decry the erosion of the liberal arts tradition—most recently seen in the critique of undergraduate history programs that do not require a course in U.S. history—the tradition remains intact.[4] From time to time, politicians question the relevance of the liberal arts to job readiness, but most CEOs, prominent politicians, and leaders in medicine and science earned undergraduate degrees in the arts and sciences.[5] Increasingly, employers view an undergraduate major in economics, history, or even English as more desirable than a degree from a professional school.[6]

A consequence of the liberal arts ideal is that students in U.S. universities have great autonomy in choosing their course of study. In other parts of the world, students are selected for particular professions long before they enroll in college. By contrast, in the United States, undergraduate students often do not settle on a major until two years after enrollment. Interestingly, students who choose their major later in their academic career actually complete their degree faster.[7]

This feature of American higher education has three important implications. The first is that students can choose courses of study based on ideas and subjects they did not experience in high school. Most high school students do not study philosophy, more specialized areas of the humanities, or the quantitative social sciences or engage in deep exploration of science. They may not have been exposed to the professions, depending on where they grew up. Few have any exposure to academicians, scientific researchers, or quantitative economists. The opportunity to expand their horizons beyond the people they meet in their hometowns has an enormous impact. The number of students who change their minds about becoming physicians is often ascribed to the difficulty of introductory science classes, but it is just as likely that these students were not aware of other opportunities before coming to college.

Second, undergraduate choice gives faculty an important opportunity. By conferring enthusiasm for their subjects, faculty who teach undergraduates have a unique forum for recruitment to their field of study.

This opportunity often gets lost as faculty distance themselves from undergraduate teaching. Only in the United States can faculty members walk into an undergraduate classroom and inspire future geneticists and philosophers who entered with no idea that they would eventually devote themselves to a new field.

Third, a curriculum anchored in the liberal arts that maximizes student choice is by definition broad-based—presided over by autonomous faculty and not rule-making administrators or government committees divorced from the academic enterprise. As a result, a college education in the United States focuses more on critical thinking and communication and less on specific vocational skills. The system is structured this way to educate students for jobs and careers that have not yet been invented.

Liberal arts faculty in U.S. universities have relatively unfettered authority over curriculum and content in courses. This is because at most universities, the liberal arts curriculum applies to all arts and sciences majors, and even students in professional schools are typically required to take a number of arts and sciences courses. Thus, the arts and sciences faculty have an enormous influence on the nature of college education.

It bears mentioning here, though it is not our primary subject, that there has been a great deal of recent discussion over a purported crisis in the humanities.[8] Our passionate advocacy for the liberal arts certainly includes a similar conviction for the humanities as an absolute requirement for the education of engaged citizens and the development of the empathy and understanding needed to navigate the world's great challenges. The so-called crisis refers often to declining majors and enrollments in humanities subjects or disagreements over whether classical texts should be valued over more modern approaches that pay increased attention to the importance of identity. We believe that what is important is the maintenance of the habits of close reading, analytical writing, and empathetic understanding of others that have not only attended the humanities throughout history but have also distinguished the American system of higher education.

Numerous studies testify to the economic benefits of a liberal arts education, but the liberal arts ideal involves much more.[9] As Steve Farmer, the vice provost for enrollment and undergraduate admissions at the University of North Carolina at Chapel Hill told us, "People look for meaning from us. I think the purpose of the university has been not just to help people make their way in life but to help them understand their lives."

RESEARCH IS CURIOSITY-DRIVEN

American universities' reputation as the best in the world is based largely on a system of research that gives academics extraordinary autonomy in setting their research agendas. No one has written about this more eloquently or prolifically than Jonathan Cole, the long-serving former provost of Columbia University. Cole's first book, *The Great American University*, lays out the history and philosophy of research institutions in exquisite detail. In his follow-up book, *Toward a More Perfect University*, he argues for reinforcing the implied compact that defines the partnership between America and higher education. Cole told us that the decision to outsource America's research to its universities was fundamental to this partnership.

Young professors first establishing their labs are not told what to study. They pursue problems that excite their curiosity and do so with little intrusion from their institution or the government. This happened because of the visionary leader Vannevar Bush, an adviser to Franklin Roosevelt, who headed the U.S. scientific effort during World War II. In response to the flood of talent that came to the United States after the war, the clear importance of science to the national interest, and the worry that scientific talent had been lost to the war effort, Bush wrote a document that established the federally funded research enterprise.[10] The principles outlined in *Science: The Endless Frontier* also set the tone for research in the humanities. The document provides perhaps the greatest description of the partnership between American higher education and the public: Bush advocated for autonomous research while stating unapologetically that the research and talent produced were in the national interest. As Cole told us, science "contributed heavily to the winning of the war, and people like Vannevar Bush, [Harvard president] James Conant, and others became sort of national heroes." In Cole's view, this produced a high level of trust in scientists, engineers, scholars, and intellectuals.

Bush was scrupulous in maintaining that individual professors or teams of professors would be responsible for setting the research agenda, and he resisted the idea of establishing a formal policy arm that would somehow evaluate the results and decide what to do with them. He worried that a hierarchical policy function would make it too easy for politicians to influence research.[11] When the American system is compared to those of other countries, we can see that he was right, and the idea of an independent agenda is what sets U.S. academic research apart to this day.

Consistent with the freedom that faculty members have to study in areas of their choice, the American Ph.D. system also assumes enormous autonomy. Graduate students are typically admitted to a department and select a research area and adviser within that department. Once they have chosen a lab (or, in the humanities, an adviser), doctoral students have significant freedom compared to their peers abroad. Although this autonomy may lead to longer terms in graduate school (or "gradual school," as it is sometimes called in cynical moments), the trade-off is that American Ph.D.s are highly skilled independent researchers, which makes them well suited for research careers in either the academy or industry.

This commitment to discovery of new knowledge allows enterprising researchers a means of assembling financial resources and infrastructure for their investigations that researchers in most other countries can only dream of. The backbone of this is the federal funding system originally created by Bush. Because the system provides little government direction, resources can follow excellent science and scientists. Although the government may sometimes initiate important programs, such as the cancer moonshot or the BRAIN project, these efforts tend to follow promising research findings by individual researchers, not the other way around.[12] There is thus no need for government committees or other bodies to decide that a particular avenue of research is worthwhile. And because there is no cap on the amount of funding a researcher may receive, American researchers have opportunities to develop large, multimillion-dollar research labs that employ teams of scientists. In more regulated systems, such as in the United Kingdom and Canada, large research groups are unusual. Further, American universities offer high levels of infrastructure support. Large research laboratory buildings are common on university campuses and particularly in academic medical centers, where clinical profits are often invested in the research enterprise. As a result, access to facilities and equipment in the United States tends to be much greater than anywhere else in the world.

The U.S. system also encourages university faculty to extend their research to the private sector. In 1980, Congress passed the Bayh-Dole Act, which requires universities to facilitate the transfer of federally funded intellectual property to the best vehicle for its commercialization. This led to the development of so-called technology transfer offices that patent university inventions and license them to start-ups or existing companies, contributing to the birth of the biotechnology industry, the venture capital sector, and the internet.

The interplay between academia and industry has created administrative overhead in the funding of the technology transfer offices and the monitoring of compliance matters, but it is a principle of American research that researchers have the freedom to pursue the commercialization of their discoveries without prescriptions from the government or the university as to the precise nature of how it is done. Thus, an enterprising university scientist can lead a large research group inside the university and play an influential role in a commercial enterprise that may have access to greater levels of scientific horsepower. This uniquely American idea of rewarding research excellence and entrepreneurial acumen spawned a set of relations among the academy, private industry, and government that forms the basis of a research ecosystem unequaled anywhere in the world.[13] By explicitly acknowledging the duty to commercialize research findings, the Bayh-Dole Act is a hallmark of a partnership that values both the autonomy of the researcher and the impact that those discoveries can have in society.

SOCIAL MOBILITY IS CENTRAL TO THE MISSION

By the beginning of the twentieth century, American universities had transformed themselves from elitist institutions designed to prepare the upper classes for careers in the clergy, law, and medicine to a meritocracy in which, in the words of the founders of Cornell University, "any person can find instruction in any study."[14] By the 1930s, universities were beginning to desegregate, and this trend was accelerated by the GI Bill of 1944. That bill, which supported returning World War II veterans, was enacted alongside the increase in federal research funding, which defined the duty of universities to produce both knowledge and talent. The advent of Pell Grants for low-income students in 1965 codified a commitment by the federal government to higher education as a primary means for social mobility.

Although rapidly rising tuition and high levels of student debt have challenged the realization of social mobility in higher education, it is hard to find an American college or university that does not place economic and social diversity among its foundational principles. Access for the next generation of American college students will be a multifaceted challenge, but by now this value is deeply embedded in the culture of most institutions. There is little doubt that the opportunity to make a difference in the lives of a diverse student body is one of the chief motivators for faculty to become part of an academic community. It is also clear that politicians at both the state and federal levels expect schools with large and growing endowments to deploy substantial sums toward making college more affordable for all. Arguably, there is nothing more important to rebuilding the partnership than facilitating social mobility.

Michael Lomax, the president and CEO of the United Negro College Fund, told us, "You've got to have been poor, you've got to have been on the bottom for generations to understand the absolute urgency of mobility. It's more than the urgency of getting something beyond a living wage. It's the urgency of economic independence, but it's also the urgency I find in our students and their families to develop themselves fully."

GOVERNANCE IS GROUNDED IN FACULTY AUTONOMY AND ACADEMIC FREEDOM

The world's first university, established in Bologna in 1098, was given a surprising degree of autonomy from the Catholic hierarchy that established it. Over time, the idea emerged that the university is an independent entity with its own procedures of governance. The original models for the American university, Oxford and Cambridge and the great German universities, largely adhered to this governing structure.

Outside the United States, many universities are controlled by a government ministry of education that promulgates governing rules and regulations making faculty and administrators state employees, precisely the situation that Vannevar Bush warned against. In the U.S. model, the replacement for governmental control—or even a rigid hierarchy of administrators—is a system of peer review combined with a system of shared governance.

Peer review involves a system in which senior faculty and other experts (the "peers" in peer review) judge the quality of academic work, and this judgment ultimately influences appointments, promotions, grant awards, and publication in scholarly journals. The premise is that the only people qualified to judge the work of scholars and scientists are other scholars and scientists who, in the words of Jonathan Cole, are "those with a high level of understanding of the field in general and the relative value of new contributions."[15]

In shared governance, which is different from peer review but related in principle, the operations of the university are governed by tenured (and often untenured and contingent) faculty in certain matters, such as the hiring and granting of tenure to faculty, the admission of graduate students, the curriculum, and the oversight of tenure protections and academic freedom. Administrators retain authority for allocation of financial resources, fundraising, strategic planning, and the administrative structure. Most faculty directives are advisory to the administration but are generally followed by thoughtful and savvy administrators. This highly decentralized and often confusing system is a distinguishing characteristic of American universities.

Also central to the idea of the American university is academic freedom. Louis Menand calls this the "key legitimating concept of the entire enterprise."[16] It is yet another part of the partnership. Without academic freedom, universities cannot effectively educate, discover new knowledge, or serve the public good.[17] Academic freedom includes, but is not limited to, freedom of expression—a concept often debated in the popular press when government, trustees, or administrators seek to restrain or discipline professors who express unpopular opinions. But it encompasses much more, including the role of faculty in determining the research and education agenda of the entire enterprise. Academic freedom depends on a high degree of public trust, which peaked at the end of World War II and has since eroded, lately at an alarming rate. The debate over freedom of expression on campus (and not just by faculty members), particularly as it relates to accommodating controversial—and generally politically conservative—speakers has brought sharp focus to this issue. The University of Chicago adopted a statement on freedom of expression that has been widely praised,[18] and many other schools have followed suit.[19] The careful navigation of these issues will be required to restore the trust between the public and the academy that has broken down over the nature of campus discourse.

THE PARTNERSHIP IS CENTRAL
BUT MUST BE REBUILT

The attributes we have discussed here describe the contours of a remarkable partnership that must be rebuilt for American higher education to maintain its preeminence. This partnership has been codified repeatedly by government actions that define the public duties of the university in producing knowledge and talent.

The problem is that not all parties understand the existence or nature of the terms of the partnership. For decades, administrators have been working with the government and trustees to define the public duty of the university but not always communicating these expectations throughout the organization. Faculty may rightly question whether they actually signed up for what is now presented as their part of the bargain. They were promised academic freedom and a role in governing the university, but they were not necessarily told that the university had made explicit promises regarding the usefulness of their teaching and research. Chris Newfield, a humanities professor at the University of California, Santa Barbara, and an erudite critic of higher education, told us, "I think faculty are focused on defending themselves against intrusive forms of accountability that seem to be changing the nature of their teaching and their research in ways they don't want." That reaction is understandable because the terms of the partnership have never been made explicit.

This is why Cole coined the term "implied compact" and why we believe that we now need to make explicit the terms of the partnership.[20] First, we need to be transparent about the promises that our predecessors have made. By acknowledging history, we remind ourselves that this is no new idea conjured up by corporate titans on governing boards—it is the same idea that motivated Abraham Lincoln, Claiborne Pell, and Vannevar Bush. The partnership is noble: it is about enlightenment and social mobility. But it is not sustainable for administrators to talk to alumni and politicians about the university's duty and not say the same thing to faculty. The two narratives of public good and public duty must be brought into conversation and ultimately into agreement. Only in the aura of this understanding can all of the parties confront together the enormous challenges that lie ahead.

{ 2

American Universities Are Challenged as Never Before

Economic data demonstrate that a college degree, by any measure, has never been more important, yet Americans continue to question whether it is worth it. College presidents have been "blindsided" by criticism aimed at the fundamental mission of their institutions.[1] Reports of continuous tuition increases over the past decade—coupled with findings that total college debt now exceeds credit card debt—have caused Americans to ask questions that were never even considered in the past: Will a college education lead to a good job and a good life? Even if it will, is it worth taking on high levels of debt to pay for it? Aside from the economics, for an increasing portion of potential college students with job and family responsibilities, the idea of committing to four years in a residential learning community is simply out of the question.

All of these factors are reflected in the numbers. In 2017, total student enrollment in all colleges and universities declined for the sixth straight year, and the decline in first-year student enrollment actually accelerated.[2] Margaret Spellings, president of the University of North Carolina System and U.S. education secretary under President George W. Bush, summed up the current environment well when she said: "We've long enjoyed a, 'Send us the money and leave us alone' kind of phenomenon. If we're so great and have a great story to tell, let's prove it."[3]

Along with their educational mission, colleges and universities are being challenged on many other fronts. According to a Pew Charitable Trusts poll, 58 percent of Republicans think that colleges and universities have a negative effect on the way things are going in the country and less than half of households making less than $75,000 a year who identify as Democrats have confidence in higher education.[4] Republican dissatisfaction stems in part from a belief that most colleges engage in liberal political indoctrination and censor conservative points of view. Democrats believe that schools cater primarily to the wealthy, are no longer accessible to economically disadvantaged students, and do not reflect the nation's rapidly changing demographics. Even university research, which has traditionally enjoyed wide public support, is being questioned by suspicious politicians as disconnected from the real world and no longer responsive to the big problems facing American citizens. Rice University president David Leebron put it this way: "If you go back 15 years, I think universities were held—not where the military is, but pretty much just below that. Now, we've fallen a lot. I think it's a very challenging time where we can't just go out in the world and say, 'We're an esteemed institution' and people will credit what we're saying."[5]

Interestingly, many of the most widely discussed economic critiques of American higher education have been convincingly addressed. First, according to a Google poll, even though the general public thinks that unemployment is higher among college graduates than it is among those possessing only a high school degree, the reality is just the opposite.[6] Second, though national student debt totals more than $1 trillion, most undergraduates owe less than $10,000.[7] Third, even though tuition sticker prices are high and climbing, most students do not pay the full amount and many elite private institutions are now more affordable to low-income students than their public counterparts.[8] Fourth, lifetime earnings are significantly higher among college graduates than among those who do not graduate.[9] In sum, college is worth it if you get the degree and do not go too deeply into debt.

Michael Lomax articulated his thinking on the value of the college degree when he told us, "There isn't a day that goes by over the last twenty years that I have been back full time in higher education that I haven't really had to think about what is the nature of the enterprise I'm engaged in. Why should students continue to pursue a postsecondary degree? What are the obstacles in their way on that path, and what are the rewards? I always . . . land on the side of this journey and enterprise being significantly more worthwhile than any of the obstacles that are placed in the way."

The furor around the value and cost of higher education obscures more fundamental problems that pose serious and, in many cases, existential threats to American colleges and universities. Indeed, colleges and universities are closing at an accelerating pace.[10] The high-profile closures of Burlington College in Vermont, Dowling College on Long Island, and St. Catharine College in Kentucky have brought attention to this phenomenon. There are simply too many schools located in the wrong places with curricula aimed at the wrong students. The fundamental problems facing American higher education can be grouped into three categories: demographics, arithmetic, and technology.

DEMOGRAPHICS

Fundamental demographic trends are changing the face of higher education in the first third of the century and causing a geographic and pedagogical disconnect between the pool of potential students and the available educational resources. A high-level look at the changing ethnicity of the nation's workforce tells the story. In 1980, four-fifths of the workforce was white. By 2020, white participation will drop to 63 percent and the share from other ethnic groups will reach almost 40 percent.[11] With the tripling of Latinx and Asian representation during this time period, the workforces of California, New Mexico, and Texas will be majority nonwhite. Much of the Latinx population—90 percent—will be concentrated in eighteen states, primarily in the West, while the African American representation in the workforce will remain relatively stable with the population concentrated in a little less than half the states.[12] For higher education, this means that student populations will be increasingly nonwhite, and greater percentages will come from the West and the relatively few states in the South and Northeast with large Latin and Asian populations. "Here in North Carolina," said University of North Carolina admissions director Steve Farmer, "growth is projected to flatten out in people graduating from high school, but the population is changing, so there [will be] many more Asian, Latina, and Latino students."

With the exception of Asian Americans, higher education in the United States has performed dismally in serving the nonwhite population. African Americans lag whites by 10 percent in the attainment of a bachelor's degree, and Latinx and Native Americans lag whites by roughly 20 percent. If these educational attainment rates persist through 2020—if anything, they seem to be worsening—the U.S. workforce will be less educated than it was in 2000 and will contain more people lacking a high school diploma.[13] This outcome is particularly worrisome in view of the increasing levels of educational attainment among our global competitors.

Other demographic trends belie the idyllic notion of the eighteen-year-old going off to the ivy-covered campus. In fact, 28 percent of college students have children, 60 percent live off campus, 62 percent work full or part time, and 38 percent attend school part time.[14] These data quickly move the discussion from one centered on the advantages of diversity and the role of higher education in facilitating social mobility to one focused on the economic imperative to educate nontraditional students. Thus, even as there appear to be too many colleges for the available supply of traditional students, nontraditional students are being underserved. The result is a shortfall in the number of college graduates the economy requires.

According to William Zumeta and colleagues in *Financing American Higher Education*, the economic imperative is clear. The jobs of the future will increasingly require postsecondary and advanced degrees. These jobs will require not only specific technical skills but also "relatively sophisticated thinking skills . . . [that allow] workers [to] use new technologies more or less continuously and to handle the organizational change that accompany them."[15] Productivity and prosperity cannot continue to grow in the United States without a steady stream of college graduates. Small, private schools can serve as laboratories for new ways to address this generation of college students, and for-profit ventures aimed specifically at this emerging cohort will undoubtedly spark important innovations. Nevertheless, Jeff Selingo, a frequent commentator on higher education, has pointed out, public colleges and universities, which are attended by 75 percent of all college students, are the only institutions positioned to handle the sheer magnitude of the opportunity the students of the future present.[16]

ARITHMETIC

We use the term "arithmetic" as shorthand for a range of financial problems endemic to higher education. To begin with, for an enterprise of any kind to be sustainable, revenue from all sources must equal or exceed expenses. Even in the world of academia—where almost any assertion is subject to debate—this fundamental premise is undeniable. Yet one-third to a half of all U.S. colleges and universities cannot meet this basic test and have little chance of doing so if they continue on their current course.[17] The causes are straightforward: (1) the ability to raise tuition indiscriminately has been seriously curtailed; (2) other sources of revenue have drastically decreased; (3) expenses have increased in lockstep with revenue and are difficult to reduce; (4) cash is scarce in many cases; and (5) traditional teaching models make increases in productivity difficult.

Tuition increases have been the first tool institutions have used to sustain their business models. Since 1997, average out-of-state tuition and fees at public universities increased 194 percent, in-state tuition and fees at public universities increased 237 percent, and tuition and fees at private universities increased 157 percent, far exceeding the rate of inflation.[18] These increases were possible because of a general acceptance of the value of a college education and readily available debt to finance it. Though not as stark as the buildup to the 2008 housing crisis, similar forces were at play. During the 2008 downturn, tuition increases began to level off at private institutions and the politics around tuition increases at public institutions became intense. Economic forces led to political pressure to keep increases down, but pullbacks in state support resulted in pressure to raise tuition to allow for continued pursuit of institutional goals.

At the same time that tuition was rising in the first decade of the new century, elite private colleges and universities began increasing financial assistance. Endowments posted large annual gains in the recovery from the dot-com bust. Median investment returns from endowments of greater than $500 million were particularly high, at 13–19 percent from 2006 to 2007.[19] These high returns caught the interest of Congress, particularly Iowa senator Charles Grassley, who began to question the tax-free nature of university endowments and the high fees paid to external managers and university endowment managers. In response, elite private institutions greatly expanded financial aid, not only to stave off political pressure, but also to recruit outstanding students who needed assistance.[20] Tuition sticker prices increased more slowly, but in fact half or fewer incoming students at top private schools pay the full cost. As a result, the net or discounted tuition rate is flat or has fallen at 73 percent of colleges and universities.[21]

Moreover, several forces have converged to place a new focus on the student's return on investment. A new federal database outlines the full costs of attendance as well as graduation rates and other relevant outcomes for approximately four thousand schools. This facilitates comparison shopping. Students and their families are paying an increasing portion of the bill for college. The percentage paid by the student is up 400 percent since 1982, which means families and students are more conscious of cost and value.[22] Some institutions have sensed this change and have begun to compete, with great success, by emphasizing their value proposition and persuasively demonstrating that a good education and a good job can be obtained for a competitive price.

Another factor that raises questions about value is the poor college completion rate. Surprisingly, only 59 percent of white students complete a college degree in six years, and this number goes down to 47 percent for Latinx, 40 percent for African American, and 39 percent for Native American students.[23] Prospective students are thinking twice about going to college and taking on debt when they see how hard others are finding it to finish their degrees.

Other factors also place pressure on the top line. State support for higher education was cut drastically as a result of the 2008 recession, with twenty-nine states contributing less to higher education in 2012 than in 2007.[24] At some flagship institutions, such as the University of Virginia, the University of California, Berkeley, and the University of Michigan, the percentage contribution of state support to the university budget is at or approaching single digits.[25] Federal research money is flat and increasingly being captured by a smaller number of institutions.[26] Even the short-term fix of borrowing until the situation improves or the business model can be revised is no longer a viable alternative for most institutions. During the recovery from the Great Recession, Moody's, the rating agency that evaluates public debt, put a negative outlook on the entire sector for two years, citing prolonged serious stress.[27] This made it difficult or impossible for most institutions to go to the public debt markets to bridge revenue shortfalls. Phillip Clay, the former chancellor of MIT, told us that the biggest long-term threat to the top line is competition from abroad. International competitors are making enormous bets on higher education, and increasingly students are staying home, threatening a significant and highly profitable revenue stream that is important to almost all American colleges and universities.

On the expense side, an alarming number of colleges and universities— perhaps one-third and maybe more—have an unsustainable cost structure.[28] The cause is relatively simple, but the solution is difficult. During the era of rapid tuition increases, institutions spent more money because they could, and they justified the expenditures in the name of school pride and a quest for competitive advantage. The increased spending appeared across the board (new departments, majors, institutes, and schools) all in the name of increased prestige, more students, and improving the brand. New dorms and student amenities made the institutions more attractive to full-pay students and their families, which resulted in application increases and greater selectivity, both of which figure prominently in university rankings. Missing from these cost increases is faculty compensation, which remained relatively flat largely as a result of the increased use of nontenure track and part-time professors to shoulder much of the teaching load.[29]

What was unclear as costs went up—but is crystal clear after the fact—is that most colleges and universities had voluntarily participated in an arms race they could not win. Each time they added a new dorm or a new course of study, their competitors countered with one of their own.

Adding to the difficulty of managing the cost side of the equation are a number of national trends. Elite schools are increasingly adopting a need-blind admissions policy in an effort to improve access for all students. In many cases, it is cheaper for a student to go to an elite private school than to attend a public or second-tier private school. For schools with small endowments that depend heavily on tuition, this development adds stress to their cost structure, and the changing demographics of future students will exacerbate the problem.[30] Full-pay undergraduates are already attending the best colleges they can get into, whereas less than 10 percent of students who need aid do so.[31] So the new students coming to higher education, especially to the elite schools, will be those who cannot pay the full sticker price. Last, the intense competition for full-pay students from abroad, often a factor that makes a school's business model work, makes it doubtful that this approach will result in sustained revenue over the long run.

The net of these factors is that institutions are running out of tricks: all of the obvious financial fixes have been employed. What lies ahead is a much more difficult path that requires a greater shared understanding of the university's duties and a more intentional effort to differentiate institutions rather than chase a common ideal.

TECHNOLOGY

No conversation about the state of higher education is complete without talking about technology. Although the craze for MOOCs (massive open online courses), discussed below, has subsided, technology will continue to affect traditional university teaching. In some respects, the basic teaching model has changed little since the founding of the early American universities. The result, not surprisingly, is scant improvement in either quality or efficiency. This has to change: students demand it, and technology, when employed appropriately, can improve learning outcomes and achieve critical economies that are essential to the survival of many institutions.

The large lecture class, especially one that is presented year after year with only minor revisions, is a historic relic that, astonishingly, still exists. In a different environment, lectures would have gone the way of record albums, print newspapers, landline phones, and network television. The typical first-year students of today rely on the cell phone as their primary information appliance, backed up by a laptop for serious research and writing. Google, Facebook, Wikipedia, and TED Talks have become their day-to-day sources of information, supplemented by hundreds of smartphone apps that summarize and curate current news and commentary. Virtually all media is seeking to push information out to interested readers even before they ask for it, ensuring that there is literally no actual news in the traditional-format newspaper or television program. When students who have been connected to the web for most of their lives arrive at their first large lecture class, they think they have traveled back in time. They typically respond by texting a friend or surfing the web, assuming that anything important will be captured by a classmate and posted to a message board or Google doc.[32]

Large lectures have become a lightning rod for criticism of higher education. If attendance is not required, students skip them in droves—even at the most elite schools—and rely on a few studious classmates to take good notes and circulate them online. Many schools capture video of lectures for students to review at a later time, leading them to skip class and simply view the lecture online at high speed. Parents and critics are outraged when they learn that university teaching is so badly behind the technology curve that, at least in some classes, PowerPoint is the only innovation introduced in the past decade.

All of this began to change in 2008, the year the first MOOC was offered. Two faculty members at the University of Manitoba decided to invite the world to join their course on learning theory by putting it online, and 2,300 people accepted the invitation.[33] Hundreds of offerings followed, and millions of dollars were invested in companies such as Coursera, Udacity, and Khan Academy as well as nonprofit consortiums such as EdX. More important, millions of students from all over the world were learning everything from computer programming to ethics, and in most cases the courses were free. We witnessed the phenomenon firsthand when our online course on entrepreneurship attracted tens of thousands of students almost overnight and each morning we could join a discussion with students from locations as diverse as Afghanistan and Brazil as well as from small towns in the United States. The technology associated with MOOCs improved almost overnight as they proliferated, and virtually every university of any size began experimenting with online education in all of its forms. For a brief moment, it appeared that MOOCs might overwhelm the traditional model of higher education, hitting a crescendo when the president of the University of Virginia almost lost her job for not being more invested in online education.

The frenzy has now subsided, mostly because venture capital has begun to run out and a sustainable business model is elusive. Still, millions of people have been exposed to a learning model that embraces available technology, and they like what they see. Online education has become an important part of the curriculum in most schools, and the private sector has embraced it as a vehicle for teaching job-specific skills. The traditional college lecture must now adapt to the lessons learned from MOOCs and other forms of online education.

Jeff Selingo told us that he didn't think that MOOCs "transformed higher education like some people claimed they would." But Selingo does believe that the MOOC craze pushed traditional faculty to do more with technology and created a sense of urgency around improving teaching and learning. For a moment, faculty were forced to confront the idea that MOOCs could replace classroom teaching. Most notably, MOOCs have proven to be an effective way to reach new populations—a development with major implications for the demographic challenges we outlined earlier in this chapter.[34]

In the short run, the challenge to the lecture model creates substantial new problems for colleges and universities. Some faculty resist the change because it disrupts a model they were trained for and requires them to re-tool their skill set and rethink their classroom. They also worry that online learning will eliminate faculty jobs in a market where there are already more job candidates than positions. Thousands of classrooms, old and new, have been built to accommodate the classroom lecture, and they are ill suited for small teams and work groups. Online classes themselves require a relatively high initial capital investment (a semester-long class could cost fifty to a hundred thousand dollars to produce), and obtaining a return on this investment requires innovative approaches that create new revenue, reduce costs, or both.

Michael Lomax believes that in today's world, we cannot let the judgment be exclusively, did you sit in a classroom for three hours a week per semester, and was the validation that you actually learned what you needed to know exclusively the validation of a faculty member? There are going to be new ways that we think about what students learn, how they learn it, from whom they learn it, and how we validate that they know what they need to know. Faculty must learn to accept that the way they are assessing what their students and graduates know is not consistently re-affirmed when students leave the classroom and go into the marketplace.

COUNTERVAILING FORCES

We can summarize the serious demographic, arithmetic, and technological challenges as follows: new kinds of students are coming to universities (demographics) with lower ability to pay (arithmetic) while institutions are seriously behind in adapting to new technology. These challenges would, in most sectors of our economy, result in rapid and fundamental change. Hundreds of colleges would be out of business, competition would cause tuition to drop dramatically, and new business models would already be adopted. Change like this has occurred in the newspaper and music businesses, as well as in retailing, telecommunications, and virtually every other major industry. Why not higher education? The short answer is that until now, traditional market forces and competitive pressures have not fully affected colleges and universities.

This is the case for a number of reasons. First, it is almost impossible to close a traditional college that has been in existence for decades (if not centuries), especially if the college has a relatively affluent alumni base. When students are granted a degree from a university, they accept it with the understanding that the granting institution will endure in perpetuity, a pact that is broken only occasionally and with great pain. The attempted closing of Sweet Briar College is a case in point. The Virginia state legislature overruled the board of trustees' decision to close the women's college, and a group of affluent alumnae temporarily provided the resources to keep the doors open. Similarly, efforts by state legislatures to reduce the number of schools in their higher education systems have been uniformly met by an outcry from alumni that make such closings politically impossible.

Still, given the economic pressures facing the approximately four thousand two- and four-year colleges and universities, many schools will likely confront an existential crisis that will produce high drama and more closings. The outcome of each crisis will depend on numerous financial and political factors, but creativity and courage to focus the mission and curtail costs will be rewarded.

A second reason that economic forces have not resulted in rapid change in higher education is that the relationship between the student and the institution is not strictly transactional and therefore economic criteria such as return on investment do not always apply. Starting salaries and lifetime earnings are only two of a number of factors students consider when choosing a college; even if economics is the primary driver of the decision, reliable information is not always available. This is particularly the case for traditional college students, who for the most part are still teenagers and are heavily influenced by such factors as prestige, sports, family tradition, social life, geography, and peer pressure.

Nevertheless, only two in ten undergraduates attend a residential four-year college full time, and nontraditional students are, out of necessity, more focused on the value they receive from a degree compared to its cost.[35] This trend will inevitably force colleges and universities to focus more on the value they are offering students and to articulate that value more clearly.

A third reason, discussed by former Harvard president Derek Bok in his book *The Struggle to Reform Our Colleges*, is that higher education has not completely shunned technological change, even if the adaptation has occurred more slowly than some feel is warranted.[36] As we will discuss throughout the book, many faculty have experimented with new technologies in the classroom, and many administrations have embraced the use of technology in new ways to enhance the student experience. Thus, the gradual introduction of new technology occurring in higher education may have postponed a more radical disruption.

Another factor has also inhibited rapid change. Until now, higher education has been held hostage to what is known as cost disease, a problem identified by the late renowned economist William Baumol as being endemic to such industries as health care and education in which economies of scale are difficult to achieve.[37] As one illustration, the average faculty-to-student ratio in a college classroom is one to sixteen, the same as in the early 1980s.[38] The for-profit education sector attempted to address this phenomenon, attracting large investments and hundreds of thousands of students with the belief that the private sector could create the rapid change necessary to educate the workforce of the twenty-first century, but the collapse of this industry has placed the onus for change back on the very institutions that privatization sought to replace.

PROMISING OPPORTUNITIES

We will develop a number of ideas to respond to these challenges throughout the book, but a few trends are well on their way to taking hold.

New Technology

Notwithstanding the high public profile of online education, 73 percent of classes are taught in the traditional lecture format.[39] Still, the success of MOOCs and online learning in general comes as no surprise to those who created and studied the emerging field. MOOCs themselves grew out of innovative classroom techniques developed by such pioneers as Daphne Kohler at Stanford (a cofounder of Coursera) and Sebastian Thrun and Peter Norvig, also professors at Stanford and cofounders of Udacity. Even before the MOOC phenomenon, a compilation of studies by the U.S. Department of Education concluded that blended classrooms—which combine online learning of factual material with in-class exercises and projects designed to apply the material—result in substantially better outcomes than either face-to-face or online learning alone.[40] Significantly, research suggests that the disparity in performance by students from disadvantaged backgrounds disappears when a blended learning approach is adopted.[41]

The reasons for the success of blended learning are clear. Material is organized into defined modules of no longer than five minutes and is followed by questions designed to reinforce the material and determine whether the student understands it. If a question is answered incorrectly, it is easy to go back to learn what was missed. Animation, videos, and other powerful visual techniques are also employed to maximize learning outcomes. When the power of available technology is employed to teach didactic material, classroom time is freed up to apply what has been learned, a combination that both improves outcomes and, if employed strategically, has the potential to reduce costs due to better student outcomes. This combination is sometimes called the flipped classroom. In reality, the case method used in business schools, many humanities seminars, and the Oxford tradition of studying with a tutor have been examples of flipped classrooms for hundreds of years.

Data analytics that recognize differences in learning styles and adapt course material accordingly are also being increasingly employed on such campuses as Arizona State University, a school with seventy thousand students. To accommodate such large numbers, the university has employed customized learning techniques (especially in introductory classes), and the result is a substantial improvement in the graduation rate.[42] As one faculty member commented, "We spend a lot of faculty time on activities that a computer can do better."[43] This same big data approach is slowly working its way into college admissions, where student data are being collected as early as the sixth grade in an effort to better match potential students with institutions that would love to have them.[44]

Internships and Experiential Learning

An estimated 65 percent of current college graduates engage in some form of internship before graduation.[45] Some schools, such as Northeastern University in Boston and American University in Washington, D.C., build their entire curriculum around external internships and actively market this differentiating approach to prospective students. The increasing popularity of the flipped classroom and undergraduate research grants means that virtually every college student will engage in a variety of active and experiential learning opportunities to supplement or replace traditional classroom time. Dartmouth president Philip Hanlon remarked to a group of faculty that learning is evolving into two separate categories: the pure acquisition of knowledge that can be achieved in a lecture hall, online, or in many other ways; and the application of that knowledge that is best achieved through hands-on active learning, often occurring off campus and sometimes with the guidance of nonacademics.[46] Like technology, experiential learning offers the promise of both improved outcomes and reduced costs as institutions share the teaching load with the private sector.

Reduced Costs

A popular view is that reducing costs is the cure-all for the problems challenging higher education. In fact, a 2016 documentary about political efforts to reform higher education is entitled *Starving the Beast*.[47] Administrative costs are often said to have skyrocketed with no apparent benefit to the school's core mission of teaching and research.

For certain, there are areas where financial discipline can lead to cost savings, but the challenge is much more complex. Although administrative costs have been rising rapidly over the past two decades, the number of executives and other managers employed at four-year colleges has been more or less flat since the mid-1980s.[48] The added staff has come in the form of other professional employees, such as computer specialists, human resource managers, and lawyers. Enhancements to student services in response to competitive pressures have also contributed to higher spending. In addition, increased regulations around sexual assault and research compliance have added considerable costs. According to a Bain report, there is almost always an opportunity to reduce costs through efficiencies and improved processes, but absent a dramatic reduction of government regulation or a de-escalation in the arms race to attract students, administrative cost cutting alone is unlikely to result in a sustainable model for most schools.[49]

Almost all schools engage in activities that are not central to their mission. Examples include computer and data services, hotels, restaurants and food services, print shops, bookstores, landscaping and grounds, power generation, and transportation services. More often than not, these activities are money-losing operations to begin with, but when the overhead associated with managing them is added, the costs often become staggering. Although there is always opposition to outsourcing on a college campus, if the case is made that the savings achieved will go to core areas such as scholarships or faculty retention, faculty and student support for outsourcing can be developed and substantial cost savings can be achieved without threatening the institution's central mission, although human and psychic costs that can attend these decisions must be weighed.

Similarly, almost every school owns real estate and other physical assets such as information technology (IT) infrastructure and power generation facilities. Techniques borrowed from the private sector such as sale-leaseback transactions and investment from private equity firms can free up substantial capital for endowment. In some cases, such an approach is simply financial engineering and makes sense if it can contribute substantially to creating a long-term sustainable financial model. Noncore real estate may also be a good candidate for a sale-leaseback transaction if the result is more resources for core activities. Ohio State University famously sold the rights to operate on-campus parking for fifty years for $483 million.[50] Time will tell whether this transaction was advisable, but similar arrangements are likely to materialize.

For most colleges and universities—whether large or small, well-endowed or on shaky financial footing—the dramatic challenges we have discussed cannot be avoided. Demographically, economically, and geographically future students will be dramatically different. Economic and political changes will continue to place more of the cost of tuition in the laps of students and their families, and worldwide competition will make it increasingly difficult to attract foreign students, who typically pay full tuition. Technological advances will present big challenges and big opportunities. There is no denying that the current system will have to undergo massive change if it is to live up to societal expectations and continue to occupy its central position at the foundation of the American experience. Any conversation on repairing the partnership between America and its colleges and universities must begin with a clear understanding of the real problems facing higher education and an open mind about approaches that may prove effective.

Applying Business Principles

The challenges we have just presented demonstrate a complex conundrum that is daunting at best. Understandably, many readers may conclude that these problems are common in the commercial sector and that the solution is to apply basic business principles that are familiar to any chief executive. Yet we make clear in the introduction and in the chapters that follow that colleges and universities cannot be run like a business. That said, techniques from the business world are transferrable to higher education so long as the foundational principles, important traditions, and established processes unique to academia are understood and respected.

The approach of Troy Hammond, president of North Central College in Naperville, Illinois, illustrates how this works in practice. Hammond, a scientist and entrepreneur, left a company in Naperville just as North Central was looking for a new president. Hammond decided to apply. He is now well into the job and thriving. In a fascinating interview, Hammond outlined some key factors to his success in building a robust student body, a first-rate liberal arts program, and a new engineering offering. First, before his interview at North Central, Hammond returned to his alma mater, Miligan College, and spent a week learning the differences in viewpoint and language between the business and academic worlds. Second, after he was selected, whenever he had a meeting with the faculty, he always wrote out his initial comments and went over them with the longtime provost to solicit counsel on how they would be heard by the faculty.

The business side of the university, Hammond said, "was easy for me," but on the academic side, "you have this completely new model of governance where it has got to be very collaborative and [where] communication and inclusion in decision making is part and parcel to coming to a solution, to coming to a plan, a strategy. . . . [You] learn very quickly that in business . . . , developing your strategy is about getting . . . the right answer. In academia, the strategy is as much about the process by which you arrive." Hammond's story illustrates that creative application of commercial principles can occur through respectful dialogue between academia and the business world. We'll address this subject head-on in the next chapter, on strategy.

{ 3
Strategy Is Critical, and Very Difficult

Business lore is filled with laudatory tales of leaders who made difficult strategic decisions that paid off. Generally, this involves a courageous choice to eliminate a business line that is part of company tradition. Killing the lunch counter at Walgreens is the most famous example, as chronicled by Jim Collins in his bestselling book *Good to Great*.[1]

Similar stories do not exist in higher education. Big choices are seldom made, and when they are, they are often reversed. Sweet Briar College was reopened after closing. The sociology department at Washington University was closed and later restarted. Countless athletic programs have been dropped and subsequently reopened. And even when tough decisions are sustained, they become a constant source of discontent at alumni gatherings. But the problems we described in the previous chapter will require a focused strategy.

Universities do not embrace strategy easily. The process involves hard choices that are typically undertaken out of necessity. In business, a strategy is driven by the changing needs of customers, competitive threats, and new technology. The fear of lost market share and diminished profits typically forces companies to make hard choices and adopt a clear strategic direction. Start-up companies typically need a coherent, crisp strategy to attract capital. Increasingly, even nonprofit enterprises are being forced by donors to make hard choices. In higher education, though, endowment, loyal alumni, government funding, and politics provide a cushion against market forces, delaying the need for a clear strategic direction or encouraging a copycat strategy that is not sustainable.

While having an original, well-articulated strategy is important for every college and university that hopes to flourish in the current environment, few schools have developed one, and even those that have rarely make it stick. The reason is clear: strategy is about being different and about making hard choices. But a university community—which is typically governed by consensus—resists direction from the top and has great difficulty choosing among competing priorities that create winners and losers.

These traits exist for good reasons: universities are permanent entities that rely on faculty governance and alumni loyalty for stability and continuity. Lowry Caudill, a trustee at the University of North Carolina at Chapel Hill, told us that the university is "built on consensus, and consensus is the enemy of strategy, because strategy is about not only what to do, but also what not to do." The problems we discussed in chapter 2 will force most colleges and universities to make hard, strategic decisions in the coming years even if to do so is countercultural.[2]

Maxine Clark, founder of Build-A-Bear Workshop and a trustee at Washington University, has seen this play out in both business and academia. She cites several reasons why it is hard to have a strategy in a university. The first is the slow cycle time. "If you tried something in the store," she said, "it would show up in the results—positive or negative— so you can act really quickly." The second is the strong resistance in academia to new ideas. "I was really surprised by it," she said, "because this is a university, where you're constantly learning." She also commented on the competition that exists among various sectors of the institution. "I didn't realize how many silos everybody worked in. I just assumed there was a lot of collaboration across the university—more than there was." She does, however, see why the university is different from retail. "When you're building brain power for the future of our country," she said, "it's not exactly something that you're going to see happen overnight."

STRATEGY IS IMPERATIVE

Academic leaders and those who support them are reasonably good at execution, especially when it comes to such repetitive events as commencement, first-year convocations, and receptions before and after athletic events. Committees that study curriculum, prepare complex grant requests, entertain high-profile visitors, and mount retirement celebrations are models of efficiency, though usually moving on well-trod paths.

In the classroom, at least until recently, a similar exercise can sometimes take place in which the previous year's lectures are dusted off, slightly updated, and redelivered.

In the academy, as elsewhere, it is much easier to put your head down and continue to do what you have done in the past, with incremental improvements. It is comfortable, for many years it has worked, and until recently it was unlikely to cause problems. The permanent bureaucracy that has flourished at most schools finds concentrating on execution an easily defensible practice, and leaders with new ideas can be waited out. As long as day-to-day activities are executed well, pressure to do things differently will subside over time.

Academic institutions that fall prey to this curse of execution may well have a strategy, but not one derived from their own unique situation. Instead, their strategy is likely to emulate a highly endowed, elite institution or engage in activities designed to move them up a few places in the rankings. Given the challenges we have discussed thus far, these strategies are unlikely to work much longer for most schools. A relatively small number of extremely well endowed universities have the financial and human resources to successfully implement an elite strategy. For the others who lack extraordinary financial resources, such an approach will result—at best—in a mediocre institution that looks exactly like its peers. Borrowing a term from sociology, Angel Cabrera, the president of George Mason University, has called this problem "institutional isomorphism," which simply means that rational actors trying to deal with uncertainty often end up producing institutions that resemble one another.[3] Similarly, focusing on externally generated rankings creates an arms race in which an initiative by one institution is countered by a similar one from its competition, leading to higher spending for all but no change in the rankings. Neither path results in the essential element required of any effective strategy: a set of activities that makes the institution distinct and allows it to achieve a sustainable competitive advantage.

The choice all academic institutions face is either to develop a strategy based on their unique qualities or to allow another external institution define the strategy instead. Taking the first approach and developing an internally generated strategy is worth the effort. Instead of simply working harder to keep up with peer institutions and a rapidly changing external environment, a good strategy functions as a road map that outlines those activities that fit and those that should not be followed. A good strategy pursued over time can give an institution a competitive edge. The curse of execution, in which the goal is to run faster and hope not to get tired, is replaced by a carefully crafted set of activities designed to further the school's overall mission and, as a result, create advantages that are hard to emulate.

Paul Friga, clinical associate professor of strategy and entrepreneurship at the University of North Carolina's Kenan-Flagler Business School, said, "You can do this [yourself] or have someone do it for you—and if they do it for you, you're not going to like it." Professor Chris Newfield from the University of California, Santa Barbara agrees. "We need to do ... [strategic planning] for ourselves and nobody can do it for us," he told us, "and I don't think we're doing a good job on that now."

STRATEGY IS DIFFICULT

In North Carolina, which supports a system of sixteen public universities, Appalachian State University and the University of North Carolina at Wilmington stand out. Formerly back in the pack with all of the schools trying to emulate the main research campuses—the University of North Carolina at Chapel Hill and North Carolina State University— Appalachian and UNC–Wilmington made conscious decisions to focus on improving their undergraduate program metrics, especially student test scores and graduation rates.[4] While the other members of the system were building graduate programs and health science initiatives, these two schools were able to distance their undergraduate programs from those of their peers and are now in a much more secure position than many other public universities in North Carolina.

We talked with United Negro College Fund CEO Michael Lomax about strategy in the historically black colleges and universities (HBCUs). Singling out all-female Spelman College, he said, "They are producing physicists, they are producing mathematicians, but they are also producing social and economic entrepreneurs. They are producing executives in the C suite." Spelman has set out to "build on openings that the civil rights movement gave to black people and the openings that the feminist movement has given to women to create a learning environment that says that a Spelman woman can compete anywhere. They linked an ambition and a determination to have unencumbered mobility for black women. They have learned in an environment which reinforced their identity, their sense of possibility, their sense of creativity." Education there seeks to remove "all the artificial encumbrances that they would argue are irrelevant to who these women are and what they have the potential to be."

On the other hand, at all-male Morehouse College, Lomax says, "the men of Morehouse have been very intentional in saying that there has to be a direct economic outcome, professional outcome, status improvement outcome related to [one's] education. But Morehouse never lost the sense of what balance they seek. What is the imprint that a Morehouse education leaves on a Morehouse man? It is a very self-aware identity of [one's] place as a black man in the world as a leader, not a follower. You do not just achieve that leadership through economic mobility, you achieve that leadership by developing a different relationship to the communities that you serve and the world in which you operate. What you are bringing is not only professional expertise, it is a sense of your role in the world as transformational."

So, if clarity of purpose works so well, why can't more schools form a clear strategy? For a number of reasons, an academic community is particularly ill suited to developing and implementing a strategy. In addition to a preference for consensus, the faculty have multiple priorities and loyalties, for example, to fields of study and research colleagues at other institutions. Moreover, a variety of very different external constituencies, including funders and alumni, must buy in to a strategy. At large institutions, it is difficult to arrive at a single strategy that is flexible enough to cover the large number of disparate activities that take place on campus.

The priorities and loyalties of the faculty often make formulating a strategy difficult. For example, a strategy designed to make an institution more attractive to federal funding agencies would be generally supported by faculty in STEM (science, technology, engineering, and math) fields but would be unattractive to those in the humanities. Similarly, a strategy built on an already strong arts program would be opposed by the STEM faculty, who see such an approach as working against their interests.

Faculty also have loyalties to their disciplines that often transcend their loyalty to a particular academic community. The creation of nontraditional departments such as identity studies or applied science might make sense as part of an overall strategy to attract an underserved student demographic, but faculty trained in traditional disciplines cannot achieve professional recognition and validation from their peers unless they work within their chosen discipline. If such a hybrid department is proposed through the combining of several existing departments, opposition is likely to be stiff.

In addition to faculty, external constituencies such as state funders and alumni have strong interests that work in opposition to a coherent strategy. How does a small state such as Maine, with a declining population, implement a strategy to streamline its system of public colleges and universities if that means that one or more institutions will have to close? The state legislators representing the town in which the targeted school is located will certainly oppose the move because a closure will harm the local economy. Alumni of the school will also oppose the move because the value of their degree is diminished if it comes from a college that no longer exists. When the University of California system responded to drastic cuts in state funding by boldly altering its economic model to accept more out-of-state students, the outcry was loud and strong: don't accept out-of-state students at the expense of those from California.[5] In North Carolina, when the state legislature agreed to reduce tuition at several state schools where enrollment had been dropping precipitously and make up the shortfall from state funds, there was strong opposition from the alumni of those schools, who thought that such a move would devalue their degrees and suspected that it was actually a first step toward closing the schools permanently.[6]

At large research universities, formulating an overall strategy is particularly difficult because they are actually multiple institutions operating under one umbrella: a graduate research university, an undergraduate institution, an academic medicine enterprise comprising multiple research, teaching, and clinical efforts, a real estate management and investment concern, and a sports entertainment enterprise that may dwarf the others in the interest it draws from the press and the public at large. Beyond these broad categories there are semiautonomous units such as a law school, a journalism school, and a business school that have particular goals that are likely to be unique to that school.

Many of these forces came together when the arts and sciences faculty at Duke University attempted to design a new curriculum. In 2014, the university charged a committee with rethinking the arts and sciences curriculum, in particular emphasizing less *what* students learned rather than *how*. After three years of deliberation, the committee's recommendations were tabled after a sequence of contentious academic senate meetings. Committee chair and philosophy professor Suzanne Shanahan said, "The nature of the opposition was largely as expected. But it also makes clear it is not in fact the right time for Duke to launch a new curriculum. A curriculum without strong consensus makes no sense."[7]

STRATEGY TAKES A CRISIS OR A VISION

Professor Shanahan was perhaps correct in the case of Duke, but in academia there is seldom a right time for a bold strategy. The Cambridge classicist F. M. Cornford, writing satirically, once said that a principle of faculty governance is "nothing should ever be done for the first time."[8] In truth, formulating a strategy usually takes a crisis. Absent an external catalyst, what emerges from most planning efforts is disappointing.

A typical scenario is as follows. A new president or dean is appointed and, after a few months of listening and building relationships, appoints a committee to develop a strategy. The committee hires a consultant from the business school or an outside firm who undertakes a set of surveys. All of the data are collected and compiled to provide an overview of the school's current situation. The strengths of the school are generally overestimated and the problems it faces underestimated. After hours of discussion and one or more off-site meetings, a vision statement is written that accommodates the needs of the committee. Based on the statement, a set of strategic initiatives is created—typically without any time frames or serious resource allocation. The strategy is announced in the alumni magazine and is well accepted because it is noncontroversial and looks very much like the strategy that scores of other schools, similarly situated, have adopted. The president and board of trustees proudly discuss the strategy, but the long-term effect is to keep the institution in line with its peers without creating waves among the school's key constituencies.

A crisis will change this scenario. Whether caused by demographics, arithmetic, or technology, at bottom the crisis will almost always involve money—cuts in outside funding, declines in enrollment, or other events that negatively affect the resources available to run the institution. For the best-endowed institutions, the crisis will likely not be campuswide but focused on a particular school such as law or journalism or, for some, the medical school and health care complex.

A survey of college and university business officers by *Inside Higher Ed* discovered that 71 percent of chief business officers believe that higher education is facing a financial crisis.[9] According to the same survey, however, over 56 percent believe that their *own* institution has a sustainable business model for the next five years; this calculation drops to 48 percent when they are asked about the next ten years.[10] Whether this finding indicates an unwillingness to face facts or an attempt to keep the bad news from important constituencies such as faculty, trustees, or lawmakers, failing to embrace a crisis as a catalyst for a strategic planning process is a missed opportunity and can have disastrous consequences.

More often than not, leadership will portray the problem as a temporary bump in the road or one that can be addressed with cost cutting through increased efficiencies. Such an approach minimizes dissent among the faculty and alumni but usually puts off the inevitable, as declines in revenue and unsustainable costs persist. The best recent example of the repercussions that can follow when colleges and universities avoid confronting bad news is the failure of most to cut expenses adequately in response to the 2008 financial crisis, which has contributed to a significant slowdown in faculty hiring.[11] Clearly articulating the bad news to those who hold the purse strings and approve key hiring decisions—as well as alumni who have consistently supported the school—takes courage, but done well, such a bold pronouncement can foster an environment for making hard choices where one did not exist.

In the next decade, most colleges and universities will likely face problems that could catalyze a bold, coherent, and sustainable strategy. There is no need to go searching for these problems. A majority of chief business officers are already aware of them even if they do not yet recognize their presence on their own campuses. Most often the problems will be financial, but intercollegiate athletics and complications arising from on-campus student life are also candidates. Moreover, according to Phil Clay of MIT, the external environment both in the United States and worldwide presents urgent issues of income inequality, the erosion of the middle class, and globalization, all of which will result in new and powerful domestic and foreign competitors. American universities will be increasingly challenged as the logical front door to the middle class and as the location of choice for international students seeking both undergraduate education and advanced degrees. The challenges will come quickly and unexpectedly, though in retrospect they will seem obvious. They will all eventually become financial problems, and no institution—big or small, highly or minimally endowed—will be immune to these global phenomena. But we believe that there is a silver lining, because the seriousness and urgency of these problems will force the kind of hard decision-making that results in a compelling set of strategic initiatives.

There is a better alternative to waiting for a crisis, and that is proactively creating a bold vision that is broad enough to inform all of the components of a coherent strategy. Michael Crow's vision for Arizona State is an example: "We want to be measured not by those whom we exclude but rather by those whom we include."[12] A revolutionary vision like Crow's has the potential to drive a wide-ranging set of activities, including admissions, curriculum, construction, and research, to name only a few. Similarly, when Marty Meehan was named chancellor of the University of Massachusetts at Lowell, he and his colleagues determined there was a significant opportunity to compete with the expensive private schools in their region. They responded with a vision that offered a high-quality Massachusetts education at a fair price.[13] The result was a strategy that produced record growth in enrollment, student retention, and funding for research and student aid.[14]

Catharine Bond Hill offered a different vision when she arrived at Vassar College. She argued that the elite liberal arts school should divert a significant portion of its operating budget and, if need be, part of its endowment to substantially increase the diversity of its student body and open itself to more low-income students. Out of this vision a strategy emerged that deemphasized student amenities, such as fancy food in the cafeteria and modern dormitories, in order to increase student financial aid, recruitment, and retention.[15] In 2017 Vassar tied for number one in the *U.S. News & World Report* rankings for economic diversity among national liberal arts schools, and students of color comprised 36 percent of the class of 2019.[16] In that class, over 60 percent of the incoming students received some form of financial aid.

Carol Folt, chancellor of the University of North Carolina at Chapel Hill, saw a strategic opportunity when she moved from an elite private school, Dartmouth College, to a public university. "The commitment to the public good, the value of the institution to the livelihood of the state, to the thriving local communities, was lasting and abiding," she said. "In private institutions, people are dedicated to the public good, too, but place is not the driver. In the public institution, place and the sense of place and the relationship to the people of a place *is* very important." Folt's vision enthusiastically embraces the sense of place and the idea that faculty who are "leaders in the world working in Kenya [are] also the leaders in the world looking at cervical cancer in North Carolina."

Employing a bold vision to catalyze a strategy has a number of advantages. The vision can be conceived and implemented as part of a thoughtful process without a set of external deadlines. It has the potential to galvanize the community around a mission that all can embrace, it is a way to align the interests of a diverse community so that everyone is "singing from the same hymn book," and it can fundamentally strengthen the institution so that it will be better equipped when a crisis comes its way.

Such a vision is created neither by committee nor by one person alone, however. One dean we know assembled a small group of distinguished alumni (the group included thought leaders, not large donors) to help him think through a vision for the college of arts and sciences at a large research university. Of course, there is never only one right vision, and one size doesn't fit all. The important things are that the vision is big and different, that it can achieve the desired effects, and that the leader advancing it has sufficient political and interpersonal capital to implement the strategy.

STRATEGY IS HARD FOR GOOD REASON

Although the discussion above emphasized the factors that make the adoption of a strategy difficult in an academic setting, many of these constraints serve a purpose. Colleges and universities cannot go out of business. The outcry from the alumni and other stakeholders will be insurmountable. This is why a faculty with permanent tenure is such an important aspect of a university. Administrators come and go, but the faculty comprises the permanent governance of the university. So although they may sometimes have narrowly focused interests, it is a good thing that administrators cannot unilaterally implement new ideas without running the gauntlet of persuading the faculty.

Further, universities have important traditions. The school colors and teams, certain highly regarded faculty members and administrators who are referred to as "institutions," some buildings that might not be functional anymore, and the grounds (especially the trees) all induce loyalty and support from alumni and campus stakeholders. Although some of these traditions are outmoded and worthy of change, the delicate way in which they are wound down is paramount.

TWO CASE STUDIES

As we discussed, thoughtful leaders have a choice when taking on the inevitable challenges facing American higher education: either wait until a crisis arises and react within a constricted time frame and with limited choices or use the looming set of threats to propose a bold vision for the future that will drive the strategic planning process. Although the advantages of acting proactively seem obvious, sometimes the only option is to wait for an external force. This is a common strategy in political and public life, and we do not begrudge any leader who concludes that waiting for a crisis is the best course. Interpersonal and political capital are required to accomplish things in the academic environment, and spending it all at once on a strategy that never gets implemented is not a productive path. Absent a proactive strategy, we do think that being prepared for an impending crisis with a set of bold ideas is warranted.

Sweet Briar College—Responding to a Crisis

A small, long-established women's college located near Lynch-burg, Virginia, Sweet Briar had for some decades operated at a deficit that in recent times had invaded its endowment at an average annual rate of 9.3 percent.[17] To try to hold the size of incoming classes at constant levels and continue to enroll students with the same qualifications, the college discounted its tuition. Beginning in 2010, the discount rate increased from 41 percent to 57 percent even as enrollment continued to decline.[18] Faced with these discouraging numbers, the new president began an internal strategic planning process that included polling of the faculty and alumni on various alternatives, including increasing the diversity of the student body, admitting male students, and adding such vocationally oriented courses and schools as nursing and education. None of the alternatives were favorably received. Although the endowment exceeded $80 million, the president and board of trustees concluded that to continue such an unsustainable business model until the endowment ran out would be morally wrong and that it would be better to commence an orderly closure of the school, which they announced in 2015.

The response was a lawsuit by alumni seeking to overturn the closure, which was viewed favorably by the attorney general of Virginia. Meanwhile, an outpouring of financial support from graduates allowed the school to keep its doors open. In the fall of 2016, the school enrolled 134 students, only 66 students short of its admissions goal.[19] The alumnae base was engaged, with two-thirds of the contributors giving to the college for the first time.[20] Bold new initiatives are being explored, including a health sciences curriculum and an MBA program, and recruiting efforts are being expanded domestically and abroad with an intention to increase and diversify the student body. The crisis that precipitated all of this change cost the school between $30 and $40 million.

Much of what happened at Sweet Briar illustrates what happens to a school with an unsustainable business model. Faculty and alumni resist change, tuition is deeply discounted in an attempt to maintain enrollment, endowment is diminished to make up the shortfall in revenue, and costs are incrementally reduced without making any structural change to the overall costs of operations. A list of strategic alternatives was rejected in favor of the status quo. Until the announced closure, the seriousness of the financial situation had never been clearly articulated to the faculty or the alumni. It took a crisis, in this case a threatened closure, to galvanize the community. One alumna active in the effort to Save Sweet Briar commented, "Alumnae would support any change if the alternative is no Sweet Briar at all."[21]

The events at Sweet Briar present a classic case study of a failure to develop a bold strategy because of the difficulty of doing so in an academic community. Absent an extraordinarily loyal and affluent alumnae base, the school would have gone the way of Burlington College in Vermont, Dowling College on Long Island, and St. Catharine College in Kentucky, which have all closed their doors. Nevertheless, it is likely that most schools will resist bold new strategies, and it will take serious near-term financial problems to drive needed change.

Arizona State University—A Proactive Approach

Established in 1885 to train teachers for the Arizona territory, Arizona State did not become a university until 1958. For the remainder of the century, it experienced steady growth in student enrollment as the population of Arizona grew; in the late 1960s, it began to grant doctoral degrees. Even then, it played second fiddle to the flagship University of Arizona in Tucson and was known best as a so-called safety school.[22]

Beginning in 2002, under the leadership of its then new president, Michael Crow, the university announced that success at ASU would be measured "not by those whom we exclude but rather by those whom we include."[23] This thirteen-word statement set the stage for a comprehensive strategic plan that transformed a middle-of-the-pack institution into the nation's largest research university. During Crow's tenure, the size of the student body almost doubled, the number of low-income students increased ninefold, the population of underrepresented students increased 60 percent, National Merit Scholars increased 61 percent, and research funding doubled.[24]

These results grew out of scores of specific strategic initiatives, partnerships, and reorganizations, all related to a radical growth strategy aimed at inclusiveness.[25] Over time, Crow's thirteen-word vision was enhanced to reflect a comprehensive charter that reads as follows: *Arizona State University is a comprehensive public research university, measured not by whom it excludes, but by whom it includes and how they succeed; advancing research and discovery of public value; and assuming fundamental responsibility for the economic, social, and cultural overall health of the communities it serves.*[26] Although these efforts did not result in a dramatic rise in popular journalism rankings, *U.S. News & World Report* in 2016 named ASU the nation's most innovative university, ahead of Stanford and MIT, which came in second and third, respectively. Education writer Jeff Selingo said, "Many universities have mission statements and so forth, but what amazes me about Arizona State is you can ask almost anybody from the highest administrator to one of the lowest employees and they know what they stand for."

The proactive approach to developing a strategy undertaken by Arizona State provides a number of important lessons. First, and most important, the strategy set ASU apart: for the first time, a university made inclusivity rather than selectivity the hallmark of its existence. Second, the strategy anticipated demographic trends in Arizona that would dramatically increase and change the nature of the applicant pool. Third, the strategy established a set of attainable expectations. Arizona State could not expect to compete with the Ivy League in some traditional measures, but the rapid growth of Arizona's population, coupled with a renewed effort to attract in-state applicants that had been going to neighboring states, made a focus on dramatic growth of the student body a realistic approach. Fourth, Arizona's climate and active lifestyle gave the university a competitive advantage in recruiting out-of-state students and new faculty, making a growth strategy feasible.

Arizona State was not in crisis when Michael Crow arrived, and it probably could have continued on its course as a middle-tier state school at least until 2008, when significant cuts to higher education in Arizona could have created irreparable harm. Instead, with a student body that had grown to almost ninety thousand and a robust research budget that was the fruit of a plan to focus on high-impact activities, the school weathered post-2008 storms by raising tuition, admitting more out-of-state students, and increasing funding from research activities.

Crow and his vision have critics. Some faculty felt excluded from the process through which these ideas were put into place.[27] Middle managers worry that they cannot enact new initiatives as quickly as Crow devises them and promises them to outside stakeholders.

Notwithstanding the inevitable criticisms, bold strategies do not often win popularity contests. We believe that Crow's experiment is important because it addresses some of the most troublesome demographic and financial issues facing higher education. It will take time before the real metrics of student success and research accomplishment can be gathered. Meanwhile, many eyes are watching the action in Tempe.

THOUGHTS ON OTHER STRATEGIES

Sweet Briar and Arizona State are two extreme examples; in reality, most schools have attributes that make them distinctive. Babson College is devoted to entrepreneurship. Reed College has a unique liberal arts vibe that appeals to a distinctive group of students. Bryn Mawr and Wellesley aim at being the very best women's colleges. The University of Chicago is known for its academic rigor (and consequently as "where fun goes to die"). Caltech has a limited scope and a small student body but, by any measure, achieves excellence.

Other universities may not have such easily discernible characteristics, but many are better known for some academic areas over others or, for example, are distinctively southern or midwestern. Most strategic planning exercises highlight such traits and recommend that schools build on them. Universities struggle to follow these plans, but the inevitable result of changing demographics, arithmetic, and technology will make it more likely that true strategies will actually be implemented.

{ 4

Students Are
Not Customers

The education of students is foundational to the idea of a university. It is why the institution was created, and from their inception American universities have placed students at the center of their mission. The founding charter of America's first public university states: "In all well-regulated governments it is the indispensable duty of every Legislature to consult the happiness of a rising generation, and endeavor to fit them for an honorable discharge of the social duties of life, by paying the strictest attention to their education."[1]

It shouldn't be surprising, then, that we begin with students when discussing the dialogue required to rebuild the partnership. All parties involved in the discussion have strongly held positions, and the cultural, financial, and political environment that surrounds the discussion makes the conversation all the more difficult. For most students and their parents and, increasingly, the public at large, a student's relationship with a college or university is largely transactional: undergraduates pay tuition, and in exchange, they expect to be prepared for a well-paying job on graduation and, subsequently, a good life.

On the other hand, the faculty might understand this charge quite differently. They would say that their job is to ensure that undergraduates are equipped to confront ideas critically, have developed skills in research, and are prepared for an examined life of learning; readying students for their first job is best left to the career services office. Especially at research universities, many faculty expect their primary responsibilities to be training graduate students and conducting research. In this view, undergraduates benefit simply from being close to the research enterprise for four years, and the spillover from this environment is what makes it special to get an undergraduate education especially at a research university.

When the college experience is conceptualized in this way, it is heretical to view higher education as a transaction or students as customers, many in the academy would argue. "They [students] want to get good jobs," says Jonathan Cole, "but they have no idea—and no one has told them—what a university education is supposed to be about, what they're supposed to find in these various rooms inside the university." Understanding and reconciling these competing narratives about students is the focus of this chapter.[2]

THE INFLUENCE OF CULTURAL MYTHOLOGY

Attending college, especially a selective one, holds mythical status in American history, culture, and conversation, and colleges large and small try to emulate their elite brothers and sisters. In Lin-Manuel Miranda's masterpiece musical *Hamilton*, Alexander Hamilton celebrates finessing his way into Columbia (then King's College), by singing, "I'm not throwing away my shot! I'm 'a get a scholarship to King's College."[3] And in the HBO miniseries *John Adams*, based on David McCullough's biography, Adams and his son John Quincy Adams engage in a deep family discussion while walking on the Adams estate during which the father chastises the son for partying too much on Harvard Yard.[4]

The allure of selective colleges imbues popular narratives about American business as well. The life stories of Mark Zuckerberg and Bill Gates seldom omit the detail that they dropped out of Harvard, implying that the degree itself is unimportant but that *simply being selected* by Harvard was significant. In fact, throughout our pop culture stories, glamorous, romantic figures attended selective colleges. In most states, the flagship institution takes on a similar aura.

Numerous studies document the outsized attention paid in media to elite colleges and universities—compared to the more than two thousand less selective, four-year institutions—possibly because many journalists working at national media outlets went to selective colleges themselves.[5] That one-third of the thirty-two U.S. presidents who graduated from college attended one of only five colleges and *all* of the current U.S. Supreme Court Justices attended law school at Harvard or Yale gives additional credibility to the mythology surrounding elite schools.

The popular focus on the elite American university casts a shadow over the process of rebuilding the partnership with the public because it badly distorts the conversation. In reality, most college students do not live in residence halls, do not attend selective colleges, and do not major in liberal arts subjects. Nearly half of all college students attend community colleges, a quarter are part-time, and a quarter are over twenty-five years old. More than three-quarters attend a college that admits over half of its applicants.[6] Importantly, many of our leaders in industry, science, and the arts do not have undergraduate degrees from an elite university.[7] Still, all too many schools try to emulate Harvard or a public flagship driven by a mythology that no longer comports with reality.

Another idea that has achieved mythic status is that a college education is the key to the American Dream. This idea gained prominence at the turn of the last century with the rise in European immigration, followed by a significant increase in enrollment at American colleges. With additional impetus from the GI Bill, implemented at the end of World War II, the narrative of enterprising immigrants and members of the poor and working classes achieving prosperity through education became synonymous with the idea of the American Dream. The idea is, "If you work hard and apply yourself, you can achieve success in the land of opportunity." The progressive immigration and college admissions policies of the middle to late twentieth century played an enormous role in developing—and in many cases, realizing—this narrative. This idea is also reinforced by a recent study showing that low-income students who attend elite colleges achieve nearly identical earnings outcomes as wealthy students who attend the same colleges.[8]

None of these cultural narratives views students as customers. Instead, they are first applicants to and subsequently satisfied members of an academic community in which membership is perceived as a ticket to a better life. This element of the student-college relationship continues to be central to the partnership. Today, though, that narrative is becoming strained as economic constraints are limiting access. As the stakes and competition to create great universities have risen, the costs of maintaining the institutions has created financial and psychological barriers, particularly for low-income students and people of color.

As stated at the beginning of our book, demographic changes produce both a moral and existential challenge—*that is, the number of full-pay, white students with high test scores in the United States has peaked.* This fact has to be confronted, and preserving the promise of higher education as the door to the American Dream for *all* Americans must be central to the new partnership.

"This is the engine for building financial security," says Michael Lomax of the United Negro College Fund.

> The abilities to think, to reason, to communicate, to engage in active learning throughout your life, those skills are the twenty-first-century skills, and to the degree that you have them, you are better positioned for the mobility so many low-income, first-generation black kids and their families are seeking. They're going through all of this labor and sacrifice because they don't want to remain poor. They don't want to remain at the bottom of society economically and socially, and they are persisting because they want mobility. They want to rise up and they know that it's not just the imprimatur that comes with an education, it's the real skills and capabilities that are going to enable them to overcome the continuing obstacles of race and class and economics which they face every day.

THE HISTORICAL RELATIONSHIP WITH STUDENTS STILL WORKS

Though the relationship between higher education and students is becoming increasingly transactional, undergraduate education is thriving in a model that does not view students strictly as customers. Entry into virtually any college or university involves applying and being accepted. If a college were a corporation and students were customers, admissions would be a simple process. Accept any student who wants to attend, and if there are excess applicants, raise tuition until supply and demand reach equilibrium. If demand is inadequate, cut tuition until enough applicants are acquired. Colleges are not corporations, however; they are, in the words of C. S. Lewis, "a society for the pursuit of learning."[9] No college or university faces a more important question than who is attracted to its particular community and who is admitted, and as the nature of the applicant pool changes dramatically, this question becomes increasingly complex.

As longtime university president Gordon Gee told us, "We need to re-establish the compact from the Morrill Act that we are for citizenship, we are for developing opportunities, we are for making certain that those who do not have access to higher education now do so, and that we take on the responsibility." These are certainly not the words of a corporate CEO referring to its customers.

Unquestionably, the demand for undergraduate education remains high. There is significant demand for spots at competitive colleges—despite all the rhetoric to the contrary—and large numbers of qualified students remain unserved by higher education.[10] Applications are dropping for less selective schools, but there is a tremendous opportunity to better match available capacity with need.[11]

The demand for a college degree makes sense. The unemployment rate for college graduates is low, generally about half that for high school graduates. According to the U.S. Bureau of Labor Statistics, at the end of 2015, the unemployment rate for all workers with a four-year degree was 2.8 percent; an associate's degree, 3.8 percent; some college, 5 percent; high school only, 5.4 percent; and less than high school, 8 percent.[12] The rates for recent graduates are higher. The Economic Policy Institute estimated unemployment rates for recent, younger college graduates at 5.6 percent and young people with a high school diploma at 17.9 percent.[13] Even for young graduates, those with a college degree fare much better.

A 2014 Pew study shows that the wage gap for college graduates versus high school or some college has never been higher.[14] This study indicates that college graduates annually earn $45,500; some college, $30,000; and high school only, $28,000. This gap is much greater than in 1979, when all three categories were within $10,000 of one another. Although some of this change is due to an *increase* in wages for college graduates, a larger fraction of it is due to a *decrease* in wages for workers without degrees. Thus, while it has never been more advantageous to have a college degree, it has also never been more disadvantageous not to have a degree.[15]

That correlation between a college degree and success in employment does not extend to the for-profit education sector, unfortunately. In fact, there is no better evidence that students are not customers and undergraduate education is not a business than the rise and fall of for-profit higher education. Strayer University, DeVry University, and the University of Phoenix have all been attractive investments in earlier times. The business model is enticing: low-income students are attracted to what appear to be valuable degrees, and many of them use Pell Grants or the GI Bill to pay tuition. The for-profit university is therefore guaranteed at least some revenue for students who have Pell Grants or almost full tuition for students who are on the GI Bill. Other students qualify for federal student loans where no interest is charged until after graduation. At its peak, the for-profit higher education business was a $30.6 billion industry, and leading companies had market caps as high as $11 billion.[16] As recently as 2012,

Mitt Romney highlighted in his presidential campaign his connection with for-profit Full Sail University.[17]

The reasons for this dramatic growth were described to us by higher education journalist Goldie Blumenstyk, who has written extensively about the for-profit sector. "They were the first to really take advantage of technology to create distance education," she said. "They were the first to create education on this mass scale and to go internationally with it; at one level, they got the access problem."

Things have changed dramatically for the for-profit sector, however. By 2015, the University of Phoenix was barred from military bases for predatory practices that enticed veterans into getting degrees of little value even as the university received $1.2 billion in tuition through the GI Bill in only six years.[18] Graduation rates at the University of Phoenix are 16 percent overall, but only 4 percent at its online campus.[19] Jeff Selingo says of the for-profit universities that "their best days are now behind them. The unfettered growth that they had—which Wall Street really wanted and investors really wanted—is just not possible without lowering quality or making promises they can't keep." Blumenstyk adds, "They had this great opportunity to be innovative, and they squandered it."

ACCESS IS FUNDAMENTAL

The earliest institutions of American higher education were founded for the wealthy. Both private and state-supported schools were designed to educate the children of landowners and the clergy. All of this changed in 1862, when Abraham Lincoln signed the Morrill Act, which marked the beginning of Jonathan Cole's informal compact between the government and U.S. higher education.[20] The Morrill Act provided land grants to states to fund new and existing universities that would teach engineering and agriculture along with military science. Although great research universities and research capacity were created, the primary intent of the act was *to provide education in useful fields to students*.[21] More precisely it stated: "Without excluding other scientific and classical studies, and including military tactics, to teach such branches of learning as are related to agriculture and the mechanic arts, in such manner as the legislatures of the States may respectively prescribe, in order *to promote the liberal and practical education of the industrial classes in the several pursuits and professions in life*."[22]

Passage of the act led to the creation or enhancement of such institutions as Kansas State University, Michigan State University, and Iowa State

University. New York cleverly added the land grant to Cornell University by including the required disciplines. The states in rebellion were excluded from the Morrill Act, but another land grant act passed in 1890 included the former Confederate states. A number of institutions now known as historically black colleges and universities were also established under the terms of that bill. Although virtually all of the land grant colleges eventually embraced research, they were originally established to promote practical education.

Notwithstanding the creation of the land grant schools, higher education remained mainly the province of the wealthy and upwardly mobile immigrants until 1944, when Franklin Roosevelt signed the GI Bill, which provided financial aid for veterans who had served in the military for at least 120 days. By 1956, 2.2 million veterans had taken advantage of the benefit.[23] The GI Bill was a boon to traditional four-year colleges, leading to greater enrollments and much greater socioeconomic diversity. Anecdotally, it is common to hear folks who were college students in the late forties and early fifties talk fondly about this period, as older, more mature students joined the universities and enriched their own lives and those of the traditional students.

The informal arrangements by the federal government to provide financial aid to students in need were codified in the creation in 1972 of the Pell Grant, named for Senator Claiborne Pell. Awarded to low-income students, this grant, which can be used at essentially any college, provides between $5,000 and $6,000 per year. When the Pell Grant was first instituted, it covered a sizable fraction of the tuition at virtually any school, but now it covers only about 10 percent of the cost of attending a private or out-of-state public university. It continues to cover a relatively significant portion of in-state tuition at public universities or community colleges.

What is important about all of these government measures is that they show a profound national commitment to accessible higher education. Moreover, although many of these measures now greatly benefit research, they all had their origins in enabling access to higher education for students, mainly undergraduates. When state support is added to the equation and the benefit of exempting nonprofit colleges and universities from taxes is factored in, it is clear that government support for students is central to the partnership with the public that governs U.S. higher education. The nature of such support going forward will be critical to rebuilding the partnership.

ACCESSIBILITY IS THREATENED

Key to the national commitment to higher education is the belief that a college degree should be accessible to all that qualify. Increasingly, this is not the case. Accessibility has two components: completion rate and financial aid. Because it is so important and so often ignored, we turn to completion rates first.

While there was a time when students with "some college" had higher wages and lower unemployment than students with no college, this is no longer the case. Because of student debt, lost opportunity cost, and the psychological damage of not finishing, students who enter college but do not graduate are worse off than those who never try.[24]

At highly selective colleges, graduation rates are approximately 90 percent. Among selective colleges, graduation rates are about 70 percent, and among all four-year colleges, graduation rates are 60 percent. Among community colleges, the graduation rate is only 28 percent, and the rate for four-year for-profit colleges is 27 percent.[25] Any discussion of the role of students in the new partnership must commit to a dramatic improvement in completion rates.

Regarding financial aid, the public universities formed either in colonial times or as a result of the Morrill Act sought to provide education at a low cost to the citizens of their states. While early on, only children of the wealthy had the time and opportunity to take advantage of public higher education, over time students from lower-income families were able to gain access. Nevertheless, state subsidies did not increase at the same rate as costs, and over time the funds from the land grants paid less of the costs.

Both public and private universities began increasing tuition significantly in the last decades of the twentieth century. In 1980–81, the average tuition at private four-year colleges was $5,594 annually, and public in-state tuition was $2,251. Today, the corresponding figures are $45,385 for private tuition and $20,092 for public in-state tuition.[26]

At the same time that tuition was rising, support for higher education, especially at the state level, was shrinking, which placed an added burden on students and their families: since 2008, state support for public universities has fallen 18 percent.[27] Adding to the problem was the increasing differential in tuition between in-state and out-of-state students, a strategy adopted in many states to increase revenue. At many selective state schools, tuition for out-of-state students is equivalent to that charged at selective private universities.

Implementing this strategy has had two unintended consequences.[28] First, the increase in out-of-state enrollment has left fewer in-state slots. Most state universities provide significant financial aid only for in-state students, so reducing the number of in-state slots works to the disadvantage of in-state students. Second, many of the students going out of state are not getting complete aid packages, and so these students are required to borrow more.

Because of the serious financial constraints at state universities, highly qualified low-income students will often pay less to attend a top private school than to attend the flagship university in their home state. At the same time that the financial burden is increasing at state schools, selective private universities are offering extensive financial aid packages. Typically, students with Pell Grants pay little or nothing to go to a top private university even though the Pell Grant itself covers only 10 percent of the tuition.

This high-tuition–high-aid model allows private universities to provide extensive aid to low-income students while still charging relatively high tuition to families who can afford it. The model works because of the high demand at selective colleges and the generosity of university donors.[29] As the partnership is rebuilt and the burden for educating large numbers of students is inevitably placed on public colleges and universities, this disparity in available financial aid will have to be addressed.

ECONOMICS ARE ALTERING THE RELATIONSHIP WITH STUDENTS

Today, 71 percent of students assume some level of debt to finance their education, making the relationship between colleges and their students more transactional than ever.[30] As of 2015, outstanding student debt was $1.2 trillion, a shocking number. Although this aggregate number is important, so are several other statistics that provide context.[31] First, 65 percent of those who owe more than $50,000 are graduate students. Second, a quarter of the undergraduate debt over $50,000 is owed to for-profit institutions. Little is known about this debt because the details are not reported in published studies. Tragically, a third of all student debt is owed by students who do not have a degree and are least able to repay.

Looking on the bright side, most students owe less than $10,000, and the average student in default owes only $14,000, making the stories of student who are $200,000 in debt compelling but rare. In reality, most private and public four-year colleges ensure that students do not graduate with large amounts of debt. The three-year default rates at for-profit, public, and private nonprofit institutions in 2015 were 15.8, 11.7, and 6.8 percent, respectively.[32]

There is healthy pressure from students, families, politicians, and the media to minimize student debt. Public colleges are usually compelled, and strong private colleges readily agree, to publish their student debt levels, thereby providing a level of transparency inconsistent with a purely transactional relationship. New government databases, as well as clever new apps, provide students more data than ever on the true costs and benefits when making a college choice.[33] Because employment levels for college graduates are high and because most colleges work to minimize student borrowing, most graduates of well-known public and private four-year colleges are able to repay their loans.[34] Whether students should have to borrow at all to attend colleges—and, if so, how much—will continue to be part of the discussion surrounding the partnership. As Goldie Blumenstyk told us, "There is an equity agenda and a financial agenda, and they don't always necessarily add up."

Even if the picture is generally more positive than the popular perception, current tuition policy still creates high barriers for low-income students. This seriously threatens the fundamental premise of American higher education as the pathway to the American Dream. In fact, large numbers of low-income students do not attend colleges for which they are qualified due to a phenomenon called undermatching, explored in a famous series of papers by Stanford economist Caroline Hoxby and Harvard professor of public policy Christopher Avery.[35] The Hoxby papers are so well known, at least among professionals who work with college access, that undermatched students are now referred to as Hoxby kids.

The advantages of low-income students attending the best possible college are obvious: graduation rates are higher, debt levels are lower, and default rates are lower. But the Hoxby papers show that 50 percent of low-income students who could qualify for admission to selective colleges actually apply to nonselective institutions, and only 8 percent apply to selective colleges in a manner wholly consistent with their academic qualifications.

Among the additional startling conclusions of the Hoxby papers are the following:

- Completion rates for low-income and high-income students are statistically identical if a low-income student attends a selective college.[36]

- Low-income status is not a proxy for race. A large proportion of the Hoxby kids are white and Asian. In fact, among Pell Grant recipients, 50 percent are white, 25 percent are Latinx, and 25 percent are African American.[37]
- Selective colleges often find highly qualified low-income students by purchasing lists of students with high ACT or SAT scores, which are not identified by income. Such contact has proven ineffective in recruiting Hoxby kids, who generally prefer staying close to home.
- Low-income students face significant barriers when applying to selective institutions, including the difficulty of visiting schools that are far away; lack of awareness of financial aid programs and related sticker shock due to the high-tuition–high-aid model; and understaffing of guidance counselors in public high schools, particularly those with low resources.

The Hoxby studies conclude that the main reason undermatching occurs is that most low-income students who are highly qualified are "one-offs"—the only high-achieving student in their school. Thus, it is very hard for selective colleges to reach them and for guidance counselors to serve them.

"If you're a rich person in this country," says Goldie Blumenstyk, "you're nine times as likely to have earned your B.A. by age twenty-four than if you're a poor person. Despite all the federal student aid we have, despite public universities, despite community colleges, despite all this other stuff we have, despite affirmative action that tends to have a correlation with income, despite all of that, it is still to me a tragic number."

Following on the work of Hoxby and Avery, Stanford economist Raj Chetty and his colleagues studied college inputs and outputs through the lens of millions of Internal Revenue Service records that match family incomes and student incomes after graduation with the colleges they attended.[38] The study produced two startling findings. First, the earnings outcomes for low-income students are nearly the same as their wealthier peers at the same schools. Hoxby and Avery found that completion rates were similar, but this is the first demonstration that actual *earnings* outcomes followed from college completion. This has dramatic implications. Up until now, colleges raised money for scholarships through anecdotes of low-income students who did well. Now the argument can be made with hard data.

Second, regional publics are best suited to address inequality. Although the earnings outcomes are not as high as they would be for graduates of selective schools, the number of low-income students who are served is much greater.[39] Chetty particularly noted the California State University system, which successfully teaches large numbers of undergraduates. Importantly, there is relatively little emphasis on research at the Cal State schools; the state already has a prestigious research university system. So the Cal State system has the three factors needed: relatively high completion rates, large numbers of undergraduates, and a focus on undergraduate education. The policy implication of this is profound: *regional publics should focus as much as possible on completion rates.*

Numerous nonprofit organizations have arisen to address undermatching. Some of these, notably Questbridge, LEDA, and Posse, seek to identify low-income students and refer them to selective colleges.[40] These organizations are extremely effective for those students who are identified but serve relatively small numbers of students compared to the total population of undermatched students in the United States. The College Advising Corps hires recent college graduates to work in schools that are likely to have undermatched students.[41] These advisers can provide greater attention to the relatively low numbers of highly qualified students in these schools.

This response to undermatching is not without its critics. Some charge that it is presumptuous to assume that all low-income students would be better off in selective colleges.[42] Those institutions are often in remote locations and inadvertently send signals that low-income students are not welcome. It is well documented that low-income students are less likely to persist in certain majors, usually science and engineering, creating academic problems if this phenomenon is not faced head on.[43] Colleges often ignore hidden costs related to social life and extracurricular activities that wealthy students pay with no problem. Attending a college with a higher percentage of low-income students does not present these inequities so starkly. The counterargument to these criticisms is that the differences in graduation rates and income expectations for students at selective colleges are undeniably better.[44]

Together, these studies provide a foundation for rebuilding this part of the partnership. On the one hand, the fact that most full-pay students are already attending colleges consistent with their qualifications means there are relatively few additional full-pay students to help address the growing enrollment problem or to provide revenue to offset the need for increased financial aid. For schools that can make available significant financial aid, the undermatching phenomenon is a great opportunity.

On the other hand, as top research universities and liberal arts colleges expand enrollment and student aid, schools with fewer financial resources will struggle to compete. Top schools will continue to get stronger by attracting high-achieving students who need financial aid, while other schools will have to work to grow the quality of their student pool using a similar strategy but without the financial resources to implement it. It is ironic that at the same time the number of students applying to college is shrinking, a sizable underserved student population is not being adequately addressed by the same institutions that are desperately seeking applicants. The institutions that muster the courage to navigate this daunting arithmetic are the ones that will survive and prosper.

Another result of the increasingly transactional relationship between universities and their students is the rise of high-dollar student amenities. Climbing walls, expensive gymnasiums, gourmet food, and funding for every conceivable student club are lightning rods for criticism. When you run the numbers, the actual costs for these so-called amenities are not on their own responsible for dramatic tuition increases or eroding academic quality (dorms and food generally pay for themselves or even make money). Such expenditures do, however, touch on important questions that go to the heart of the relationship between universities and those who support them and raise a more fundamental question posed by students, parents, policymakers, and taxpayers alike: What are they are getting in exchange for their tuition and tax dollars? The answer will be different for every school, but straying from an institution's core mission and values will exacerbate the already frayed relationship with many of its most important constituents.

STUDENTS AND THE NEW PARTNERSHIP

As the parties come to the table to begin rebuilding the partnership, classifying students as customers is both erroneous and dangerous: erroneous because, as we hope we have demonstrated, students are selected to become part of a learning community rather than being merely customers engaged in a commercial transaction; dangerous because most institutions that have treated students as customers—most notably for-profit universities—have failed by any measure. Nevertheless, faculty and administrators can do much more to build the learning community most students seek and to make that community unapologetically intellectual while at the same time meeting students' legitimate expectations.

{ 5

Faculty Are
Not Employees

At the heart of the partnership that makes American universities great is an understanding of the role of faculty. Faculty teach and participate in the governance of their institutions; in research institutions, they are also expected to be active scholars in their disciplines. Tenure, academic freedom, and taking a role in the governance of their academic community are aspects of their profession that contribute to making the university unique and enduring.

Faculty prerogatives such as tenure and the freedom and job security that come with it are controversial, but even those who understand and support this unique relationship with faculty expect teaching and research—as well as responsible governance—in return. In this chapter, we explain the implicit bargain that establishes faculty not as employees but rather as members of an academic community who are expected to assume responsibilities for the public good in exchange for an unusual level of freedom and autonomy.

EVERYONE TEACHES

We begin with teaching because, after all, educating students for a productive life is why colleges were created in the first place. To rebuild the partnership with the public, faculty must teach. Students, parents, governing boards, legislatures, and the public at large all expect professors, no matter how illustrious their credentials and how important their research, to devote a portion of their time to teaching both graduate students and, especially, undergraduates. This applies to administrators as well. Everyone who occupies faculty status carries an obligation to participate in the university's most important function. The erosion of this understanding through the growing abdication of undergraduate teaching by tenured faculty is highly corrosive and must be addressed. At the same time, the marginalization of nontenured faculty, who undertake an increasing percentage of undergraduate teaching, is producing an untenable situation.

A large part of the negative perception of American higher education grows out of a belief that faculty are not living up to their end of the bargain when it comes to teaching. Across the board only half of undergraduate courses at public two-year and four-year colleges and universities are taught by full-time tenured or tenure-track faculty.[1] The statistics become even more alarming when only research universities are measured because a light teaching load is considered a necessity by the high-profile researchers that schools are eager to please, especially those who have been courted by other universities.[2] Moreover, as academics move up the hierarchy into administration, their paychecks go up but their teaching loads disappear. The hole these phenomena create is filled with nontenure-track full- and part-time faculty (called fixed-term faculty), administrative employees who have academic credentials (so-called alt-acs), graduate students, and postdoctoral fellows.

The problem with this arrangement is both real and perceived. The real problem is that these contingent faculty members are underpaid and underappreciated. The problem in perception is that outsiders believe—because we tell them on admissions tours and in brochures—that the tenured faculty are superior teachers. And that may be true in many cases, but fixed-term full-time professors are often among the best teachers on campus.[3] Teaching is their top priority, and they commit time and energy to developing new forms of pedagogy and helping other faculty improve their teaching. Depending on the policies of the institution, they often fill important positions in faculty governance and routinely win teaching awards. They seldom are rewarded with named professorships, and therefore their compensation is substantially below that of tenured faculty. But they make a commitment to the mission of teaching, and most universities, of all types, could not function without them.

This misperception can be remedied in part by improving compensation for fixed-term faculty and creating named professorships explicitly for teaching, but such steps do not eliminate the need for senior faculty and administrators to shoulder their share of the teaching load. If teaching is central to the bargain that makes American higher education great, the actual task of teaching cannot be largely outsourced while the elite scholars pursue their research, make administrative decisions, and train a handful of graduate students. Moreover, professors and administrators cannot effectively perform their roles in institutional governance and administration if they are not in touch with students. Teaching, especially undergraduate teaching, is the only way to do this.

Regarding administrators, a host of compelling reasons can be advanced for why they do not have time to teach. Nevertheless, the effect of the leaders of a college or university embracing a teaching role can be profound. In fact, it is doubtful that the faculty will meet the expectations of the public unless the best-known administrators and professors assume a highly visible teaching role. Michael Roth, president of Wesleyan University, teaches a set of widely acclaimed courses,[4] and Jonathan Cole told us that he continued to teach while provost at Columbia. When Holden was the chancellor of the University of North Carolina, the two of us taught an introductory course on entrepreneurship in the department of economics to more than two hundred students. That course also evolved into a MOOC with an enrollment at one point of more than forty thousand students. As provost of Washington University, Holden teaches a seminar every year on higher education, along with a summer course for promising low-income high school students in St. Louis. At WashU, vice chancellors and other administrators have also reentered the classroom.

So if tenured faculty and administrators aren't teaching enough, who is teaching? A large part of the burden is carried by part-time adjunct professors—who are poorly paid and often required to teach at multiple institutions to make ends meet—postdocs, and graduate students. They have no time to participate in faculty governance and in many cases no time to meet with students outside of class. They are paid to fill holes in course offerings, meet demand in popular subjects, and otherwise hold the teaching mission together for compensation as low as a few thousand dollars per course and often with no benefits. These faculty and graduate students are understandably beginning to insist that they are employees, and increasingly they are being legally recognized as such. Adjunct faculty have been affiliating with labor unions since 2013, and in 2016, graduate students at private universities were given the right to unionize as well. Whether or not they belong to a union, these teachers should not be misclassified to their disadvantage.

EVERYONE MUST TEACH WELL

The partnership is also under scrutiny when it comes to *good* teaching. Merely encouraging faculty to teach is not enough. Students, their parents, and the public at large are asking two fundamental questions: What should be taught, and what is the best way to teach it? When it comes to content, the economic insecurity that has lingered long after the Great Recession—combined with high tuition and individual reluctance to take on debt—have prompted almost all colleges and universities to integrate such real-world skills as collaboration, team building, and critical thinking into their curriculum. Increasingly, though, students want even more. Students want a credential that readily translates into a job in addition to a liberal education that will last a lifetime. Academics react to this insistence on immediate relevancy with concerns that their institutions are becoming glorified trade schools and that their graduates will be ill equipped for a rapidly changing world in which the best jobs have not been invented yet. Worried about their bottom line and increasing competition, administrators attempt to fulfill students' demands with enhanced career services and new curricular offerings.

Ultimately, every institution will resolve these competing priorities in different ways, but the partnership requires that college prepare students for a useful and productive life that blends both the skills and the habits of mind embodied in the liberal arts and sciences with exposure to practical skills and experiences that can be learned only through interaction with the world outside of academia. "Not everyone is an excellent teacher," says West Virginia president Gordon Gee, "but everyone needs to have relationships with students, and those who are teaching and teach well need to be rewarded." Gee points out that there is an ethic that says that if you aren't a good researcher, "at least you can teach—well, hell, that's wrong, that's the wrong message we're giving out."

Providing a practical set of skills tailored to a specific entry-level job does not in and of itself constitute a college education, and this is being increasingly recognized in the marketplace, where liberal arts majors earn more over a lifetime than many who major in more technical subjects.[5] In our own experience, providing some level of job-related skills and experience, such as internships and interviewing techniques, as a complement to a traditional academic course of study is a productive approach. Students gain the unique benefit of deep exposure to one of the traditional academic disciplines while also gaining a pathway toward an entry-level job. Even for those committed to a more vocational degree, such as journalism or nursing, it is important to supplement real-world skills with a core curriculum in the arts and sciences so that graduates have the intellectual foundation necessary to participate fully in the rapid economic and social change they will experience during their lifetimes.

The harder question is how best to teach. We start with a basic premise. The traditional lecture model, in which a professor stands in front of a class and talks for an hour, needs improvement. Sanjay Sarma, who heads digital learning at MIT, puts it this way: "It's like Al Gore's inconvenient truth. We have conveniently assumed that the student is a sheet of paper [and] a professor has a pen. The professor [can] sit down and [for a hundred students] write in their brains, declare victory, and the students have learned. This is a false notion. . . . We have assumed that if a student can memorize and regurgitate . . . on an exam we can . . . wash our hands off and assume they have learned."

Sarma goes on to argue that hard data prove that students need to learn slowly and repeatedly and then actually *use* the material both intellectually and physically, often with their hands and ideally in connection with a project related to the real world. He also suggests that learning is best when it is "just in time" and is associated with solving an actual problem, as opposed to being used in a thesis two years after the learning takes place.

Although Sarma is based at perhaps the greatest technology institute in the world, he believes pedagogy comes first; once we understand how students learn, developing the tools to facilitate the process is the easy part. He puts forward the example of a flight simulator. Without such a tool, it would be impossible to train pilots in large numbers because training would be essentially a one-on-one experience in a real airplane. A simulator reproduces actual in-air experiences with a master pilot teaching an apprentice the subtle lessons that can be so critical in a crisis. Young pilots can apply and practice those skills over thousands of hours with immediate feedback from the simulator itself, supplemented with practical hints from instructors.

Sarma's ideas are already finding their way into the wider culture with the popularity of do-it-yourself videos on virtually every subject on YouTube and other similar platforms. Cookbooks are now deconstructed into videos so that recipes can be viewed just in time over mobile phones when they are actually needed, and the baffling task of tying a bowtie is made simple in a demonstration by a social media personality.

Little of what we've learned from flight simulators and YouTube has found its way into the college classroom, however, for a variety of reasons. As Sarma's research demonstrates, merely taking good notes and regurgitating the information on an exam does not amount to learning. But a continued reliance on the traditional lecture model makes it tempting for some instructors to eschew large revisions to their courses, leaving more time for the research that garners them acclaim and professional advancement. Many professors are also suspicious of technology in the classroom and of the motives of its advocates.[6]

Students, too, resist change in the traditional lecture model. They have been brought up on the traditional passive learning approach, and so were their parents. Sarma says students that assume a good grade in a class means they have mastered the material, and they have little experience with the real learning that occurs when an experiment fails or a proposed enterprise is met with disdain by potential customers. As a result, they often resist innovative approaches such as learning simulators and online lectures because they feel they are not getting appropriate attention from a "real" professor. Parents are concerned they are not getting their money's worth if technology replaces a live professor.

The third factor that works against innovative learning is a general resistance to change among the various members of the university community. Notwithstanding empirical data that show that the traditional educational model is broken, it will take outside forces to bring a wholesale embrace of new models for learning.

We believe that such forces are already in play. The demographic and economic threats facing the majority of colleges and universities will force change in the learning model. The old model simply does not scale, and—although scaling new models still requires more innovation—shifting attitudes toward online education, driven by the popularity of Khan Academy, TED Talks, YouTube, MOOCs, and the like, have already resulted in greater interest and acceptance of online learning, especially when it is supplemented with in-person experiential learning.[7] Impressive data have also been gathered on the superiority of new models that better integrate technology inside and outside of the classroom.[8] Ultimately, to continue to uphold their end of the partnership, professors must redefine great teaching so that technology is employed not in the name of efficiency but in an effort to achieve better learning outcomes.

FACULTY MUST ENGAGE WITH THE PUBLIC

Along with great teaching, public engagement is central to the bargain with the American citizenry. Research is a big part of such public engagement. Nevertheless, beyond the specifics of technology transfer, company creation, and economic development, a more fundamental expectation must be explicitly acknowledged and addressed if the partnership is to endure. In exchange for the unprecedented freedom granted faculty to pursue their research and other intellectual interests, professors must meet the public halfway and contribute to the public good, broadly defined.

This is a fundamental value as old as the American university itself. The charter of the first American public university refers to the "social duties of life," and the Morrill Act of 1862 codified a trade of land and public support for land grant universities in exchange for explicit services aimed at the public good.[9] Vannevar Bush restated the bargain in 1945. Interpreting this obligation in a contemporary context is essential to rebuilding the partnership. Certain principles should frame the discussion.

First, the potential for discoveries that will benefit society is an important consideration when academics undertake research or other activities. Academics recoil when administrators talk about this sort of impact for their work, feeling that it demeans their research. Impact need not mean an immediate pecuniary result; it could result in benefits later on. To reassure the faculty, administrators must continually remind the public that basic research in the sciences may not pay off for years and that fundamental research in the humanities and social sciences has never been more important as understanding culture and the human psyche increase in influence.

Still, although the exact percentages are subject to debate, most published articles in the humanities are never cited in the work of other researchers, and many scholars in the humanities are hard pressed to find public outlets and interest for their work. In the social sciences and medicine, where the culture of citation and commenting on published work is well developed and important in the validation of new knowledge, 70 percent of articles in the social sciences and about 90 percent of papers in medicine get cited in the work of others.[10] Notwithstanding this general low incidence of citation in fields other than science, the number of academic journals continues to increase, from thirteen thousand fifty years ago to seventy-two thousand today.[11] Although it is not fair to say that all uncited or still-unread articles are without value to society, the inescapable conclusion from the data is that a significant amount of academic research is undertaken without regard for the size of its audience. While this may be impossible to determine in advance, the press and the public at large are taking note of this aspect of research, and it is reasonable to assume that the relevance and impact of academic study will be of increased consideration in rebuilding the partnership.

Faculty also have a responsibility to be accessible across their professional lives. The obvious example is the expectation that faculty will engage with students outside of class in formal and informal settings. No matter the size of the school and the subject matter being taught, knowing and interacting with faculty is an important part of a college education, but this has become increasingly difficult in an era of large classes and multiple demands on faculty time. Combined with the increased use of part-time instructors and adjunct professors who might teach at several institutions, this important part of the learning experience is threatened.[12]

The engagement of academics with the public is essential if the university is to sustain the partnership. In a talk to the Council on Competitiveness, futurist and tech luminary Bran Ferren challenged the members of the audience who were not in academia (the council consists of representatives from university administration, corporate CEOs, and organized labor) to name a living scientist.[13] Nobody could do it. This is untenable, and the problem extends to the social sciences and humanities, where public scholarship is arguably even more important.

We believe two problems have to be solved. The first is the inability of the university to facilitate public engagement for academics. Some might say that the problem is that faculty are simply inaccessible; certainly, that is part of the issue. Nevertheless, by rewarding specialized research and not providing coaching and opportunities for public engagement, universities are not incentivizing faculty to engage with the public.

The second problem is that there is sometimes a powerful disdain in the academy for public intellectualism. Carl Sagan was famously not voted into the National Academy of Sciences, and some historians bristle when alumni tell them how much they love David McCullough and Lin-Manuel Miranda.[14]

Academia could learn from the great ballet companies and symphony orchestras. Even the New York Philharmonic does Christmas concerts and cinema nights in which the orchestra plays the soundtrack of a popular movie; the New York City Ballet still stages *The Nutcracker* and *Swan*

Lake. They do this because they need the money but also because they are committed to building the audience for classical music and ballet. Similar behavior is not well received in academia: presentations by faculty to the public are often viewed as distractions from their more important research work, and the publications of faculty who undertake public scholarship are not highly valued when decisions about tenure and promotion are made.

The three ideas we have just discussed—teaching, teaching well, and public engagement—usually do not sit at the center of the financial rewards for faculty. Most financial rewards come for success in research. Although we hope that many will be motivated by concern for the health of their disciplines, their institutions, and for higher education itself, administrations and trustees still need to wrestle with new ways to provide financial incentives for these behaviors that enhance institutions in important ways.

TENURE IS CONTROVERSIAL BUT ESSENTIAL

In American universities, the quid pro quo for teaching, undertaking research, and engaging with the public is a set of privileges little equaled in other walks of life. This is the other side of the partnership between the faculty, the university, and the public at large. It involves tenure and the related concepts of academic freedom and shared governance— among the most contested matters in all of higher education. There are misconceptions outside the university about these privileges, but even when they are understood, outside stakeholders resist and even resent these foundational principles. Yet so long as the faculty upholds its end of the bargain, there are persuasive arguments for this set of ancient faculty prerogatives that combine to make colleges and universities enduring institutions. Equally important, but not generally appreciated, tenure is a remarkably cost-efficient tool for recruiting and retaining faculty. Without it, the economics of higher education would be in even more serious peril.

Legally, tenure is a property right that is stronger than a contract. It is extremely difficult to dismiss faculty who hold permanent tenure. The precise nature of tenure protections at a given institution is typically laid out in a document published by the university. Modifications to the tenure document generally require a faculty vote and possibly approval by the legislature or governing board. The tenure document describes a set of procedures by which actions, including termination, can be taken against a tenured faculty member. In these cases, a group of peers hears the charges and makes a recommendation to the administration. The recommendation is generally advisory, but in practice, the advice of these committees is typically followed. A breakdown in the due process rights of tenured faculty has the potential to create a difficult crisis for a university. Fixed-term faculty generally enjoy the same protections as tenured faculty for the term of their contract.[15]

Legal challenges to the absolute protections of tenure have typically produced results quite favorable to the faculty member. For example, in 2015, Paul Frampton, a professor at the University of North Carolina, was awarded back pay for the time he was imprisoned in Argentina on drug charges.[16] Trustees at the University of Illinois settled a court case with Steven Salaita, who claimed that he was owed compensation after the university rescinded a job offer. Salaita was offered a tenure-track position by the university, subject to final approval by the board of trustees, but the chancellor revoked the offer after reviewing a series of Salaita's tweets that raised concerns at the university about their decision to hire him. An Illinois court found that trustee approval was a formality, ruled that Salaita was essentially already a faculty member entitled to tenure protections, and awarded him compensation of more than $800,000.[17] Because of cases like these, universities typically seek out-of-court settlements with tenured faculty they wish to terminate, much to the consternation of trustees and legislators negatively inclined toward tenure in the first place.

Though difficult, it is possible to dismiss tenured faculty, usually for neglect of duty or misconduct. Such decisions are typically made by administrators, but they can be appealed to a faculty hearings committee. These faculty hearings are generally advisory, and in theory administrators have the prerogative to ignore the result. In practice, administrators seldom ignore such rulings because if the faculty feel that administrators have lost respect for shared governance, it is hard to build needed consensus on other matters.

Many universities have adopted a system of post-tenure review. In this system, a faculty committee reviews the performance of all tenured faculty at some regular interval, typically every five years. The committee can find that a faculty member's performance is deficient in some way and recommend a plan for enhancing the contributions he or she is making. This plan can be used either to encourage and measure activity or to provide an entry into a discussion about retirement. At some universities, failure to follow the development plan produced in the post-tenure review can be seen as neglect of duty and grounds for dismissal.

Tenure has endured for so long because, counterintuitively, it is a remarkably cost-efficient system for recruiting, compensating, financing, and governing the most distinguished faculty. First, consider recruitment. When a university advertises a tenure-track position, it typically receives hundreds of applications. These applications are from individuals who have completed four to ten years of graduate school and often two years or more of postdoctoral research. The starting salaries for these positions range from $60,000 in the humanities to $80,000 in the sciences and up to $150,000 in economics and the business school. These applicants are being attracted not by a high salary or even the prospect of a high-paying job in the future but rather by the possibility, though still remote, that they might eventually secure a tenured position—in effect, a lifetime appointment—that would give them the economic security and intellectual freedom to pursue scholarly research and teaching.

Second, the economics of tenure are compelling. For what other job would people train for years in order to earn $60,000—even after beating out more than a hundred other candidates for the job? Once a faculty member is hired in a tenure-track job, they have roughly six years to compile a dossier to support the granting of full tenure. This time is typically among their most productive in both research and teaching, and the prospect of tenure certainly contributes to such productivity. The compiled dossier is subject to extensive internal and external review before a final vote of the tenured faculty is taken. The rate at which tenure is granted varies widely among institutions, but the chances can be remote at some schools. When not granted, the candidate usually moves on, thereby creating an opening for the process to start over with another highly talented and incentivized candidate hoping to achieve his or her academic dream. The granting of tenure usually comes with a relatively modest raise in financial compensation. The huge applicant pool, the relatively low starting salary, the strong incentives for productivity, and the extended and comprehensive evaluation period combine to create a near-perfect economic model as far as the university is concerned.

Gene Kahn is a long-serving trustee of Washington University who had a distinguished career in retail, including serving as the CEO of the May Company. Kahn told us that without tenure, "the professors would always be concerned about their ongoing employment, but it really allows us to sustain our relationship with our top academic leaders." Kahn has noticed in meeting with pretenure faculty members how preoccupied they are with their precarious employment status. The granting of tenure relieves faculty of their fears of being let go in exchange for an appointment to a life of scholarship and teaching. Kahn acknowledges that not all tenured faculty remain productive for their entire careers, but "it allows us to have a collection of the greatest thinkers and educators, and that is how the university propels itself."

Tenure also provides long-term stability in university governance. Universities are engineered to be long-established institutions that do not go out of business. The careers of administrators have become more contingent and precarious in recent years, however, leading to shorter terms of service for provosts and presidents. As a result, the tenured faculty is often the de facto leadership of the institution. The presence of tenured faculty with significant influence over the operations and major decisions of the university protects against the possibility of short-term administrators making decisions that place the university in peril.

Said another way, the tenured faculty are the conscience of the institution. The protections of tenure and the ideas of shared governance allow the faculty to assume this role and provide a check on short-sighted decisions by administrators and board members. A good example of this principle in practice is when the faculty governance apparatus at the University of Virginia questioned and ultimately aided in the reversal of the abrupt and ill-considered decision by the board of trustees to dismiss President Teresa Sullivan in 2012.

It is undeniable that some academics remain in their positions long after they have stopped being productive in research and often when their teaching is no longer exciting. Nevertheless, the economic advantages of the overall system far outweigh the costs incurred at the end of some faculty careers. In addition, there are methods to encourage faculty members to retire, including buyouts involving one-time, lump-sum payments and phased retirement programs in which professors drop to half-time and half-salary for some predetermined period in exchange for relinquishing tenure.

Resolving issues surrounding the balance of teaching and research, tenure, and shared governance will necessarily be part of any attempt to rebuild the university's partnership with the public. If faculty agree to do more teaching, to work to publicize their research, and to at least be supportive when administrators talk about the need to consider the wider impact of their research, then there is a better chance that the public will understand why tenure, academic freedom, and shared governance are necessary. We believe that this handshake is one of the most important factors in sustaining American universities, and it is the essence of answering the higher calling.

University Leadership—
More Complicated and
More Critical Than Ever

On June 7, 2012, at 9:06 P.M., the rector of the University of Virginia, Helen Dragas, sent President Teresa Sullivan an email asking her to meet Dragas, along with Vice Rector Mark J. Kingston, the next day.[1] At the meeting, Sullivan was told that "a majority of the board [were prepared to unseat her], that she had no support within the faculty, and that it would be better that she resign than face a board meeting and the ensuing public controversy." She was asked for an answer within twenty-four hours. Although the demand came as a total surprise to Sullivan and no specific reasons for the resignation request were given, she proffered her resignation and the board accepted it on June 10, effective August 15, citing "philosophical differences." Dragas followed up with a communication to a group of vice presidents and deans to say that financial conditions were forcing reallocation of university resources in line with a "passionate articulation of a vision and effective development efforts to support it." She further stated that "higher education is on the brink of a transformation now that online delivery has been legitimized by some of the elite institutions." Finally, she stated, "We do not believe we can even maintain our current standard under a model of incremental, marginal change. The world is simply moving too fast."

Over the next seventeen days, the UVA community was thrust into turmoil. At an emergency meeting of the faculty senate on Sunday, June 17, Provost John Simon stated, "I am now wondering whether my own beliefs about the values of higher education are consistent with our Board. The Board's actions over the next few days will inform me as to whether the University of Virginia remains the type of institution I am willing to dedicate my efforts to help lead." In that meeting, the faculty senate voted "no confidence" in the board of trustees.

At a closed meeting of the trustees the next day—with a crowd of thousands on the steps of the Rotunda, where the meeting was held— President Sullivan set forth a detailed response to the board's concerns, stating, "I have been described as an incrementalist. It is true. Sweeping action may be satisfying and create the aura of strong leadership, but its unintended consequences may lead to costs that are too high to bear. Corporate-style, top-down leadership does not work in a great university."

Rector Dragas responded the next day in a statement that said, among other things, "The days of incremental decision-making in higher educa-tion are over," in light of cuts in governmental support, "the coming tsu-nami" of online learning, and a rapidly changing health-care environment. She also suggested that the university's "approach to securing gifts and grants . . . seemed to be adrift, lacking a specific vision and plan." Other critics piled on, most notably hedge fund titan Paul Tudor Jones, an alum and the university's largest donor, who wrote an op-ed in the *Charlottes-ville Daily Progress* stating that "UVA needs proactive leadership to match the pace of change."[2] Nevertheless, faculty and students rallied to Sullivan's defense and the governor threatened to dismiss the entire board if it did not unite on a plan. On June 26, in the face of concerted pressure from the university community as well as alumni and the regional press, the board unanimously reinstated Sullivan as president.[3] She continued to serve as president until her voluntarily announced retirement date of June 30, 2018.

We begin with the firing and subsequent rehiring of Terry Sullivan not because it is typical or is likely to happen often but because the story dra-matically illustrates the complex internal and external challenges facing administrators and board members as they negotiate the important issues facing higher education. We use the term "negotiate" intentionally because in a learning community, the development of consensus is particularly important. As a result, the president of a college or university functions more like a politician than a corporate CEO, and the board functions more like an oversight committee than a traditional corporate board, although the board has certain clear corporate duties that we describe below. As events at Virginia illustrate, the views of faculty, staff, students, alumni, and politicians have enormous influence, especially when they act collec-tively. On fundamental issues, the power of these diverse constituencies often exceeds the formal power of either the president or the board of the university. This is particularly the case in the current environment in which boards of trustees and government bodies are becoming more deeply involved in the actual operations of the institutions they supervise.

The difficult, time-consuming process of achieving consensus around fundamental university issues is understandably frustrating, especially to university trustees who come from the private sector. The Terry Sullivan incident illustrates the value of the process. The UVA board may have underestimated the influence of the various constituencies of the university, but they were on the right track in terms of the threats to the university caused by rapid change. Although the school's financial situation was not as serious as the rector portrayed it, reductions in state support and market-driven limitations on tuition increases did require a degree of prioritization that is countercultural at schools like Virginia. Similarly, although MOOCs were in 2013 the next "new thing," it was far from clear that MOOCs would be the means by which technology would revolutionize higher education. In fact, subsequent events would show that MOOCs were only part of a larger movement to change the traditional lecture method.[4] Ironically, Sullivan—with her administrative experience as provost at Michigan and the institutional support that she had obviously accumulated over her tenure at Virginia—was precisely the right person to manage the budget and incorporate the lessons learned from the early days of online education into the university's overall strategy.

In this chapter, we explore the complex relationship between a university's board and its president and suggest a framework for what is required of the university leaders of the future if they are to rebuild the partnership with the public. We begin with a fundamental belief that universities are not corporations and cannot be run like one, and that the system of university governance that has evolved in the United States, with all of its shortcomings, is what makes American higher education great. We further believe that if all parties understand the workings of university governance and respect the process that has evolved, the important decisions that lie ahead can be made in a manner that preserves the idea of the great American university and the system of higher education that idea has fostered.

A UNIVERSITY PRESIDENT IS MORE LIKE A POLITICIAN THAN A CEO

Bart Giamatti's description of the job of college president is worth remembering. He called it "a mid-nineteenth-century ecclesiastical position on top of a late-twentieth-century corporation."[5] The modern research university requires the president to manage large annual budgets often exceeding a billion dollars, to oversee thousands of employees, to negotiate and maintain sizable contracts with large corporations, to run hotels, to manage police departments, and many other activities that require a president's authority. Leaders of any college or university encounter similar challenges, although typically on a smaller scale. But in all, the nature of a learning community demands leadership largely by consensus, requiring a leader to maintain political capital with constituencies as diverse as Nobel Prize winners, political activists, accomplished athletes, and dedicated grounds employees. Further, the very board members who expect decisive and practical leadership from the president also expect the president to hold forth on all of the academic areas of the university. Holden is fond of telling his new hires that university administrators are expected to think like Stephen Hawking and talk like Jack Welch.

As the Sullivan affair illustrates, a college president occupies a relatively tenuous position. Terry Sullivan was fired in the middle of the night for reasons unknown to her but that may have been based more on her leadership style than on substance. What saved her—the support of the faculty, students, and other internal groups—has proven to be the undoing of others. At the University of Missouri, the dissatisfaction of the deans with the chancellor was a key reason for his departure.[6] Larry Summers had a relatively short term as the president of Harvard because of dissatisfaction within the faculty of arts and sciences.[7]

Fundamentally, the president must represent the various constituencies internal to the institution to the board and the outside world, and to do that, academic processes and sensibilities must be respected, while at the same time a complex institution must be run efficiently. Adding to the challenge, most institutions—rightfully in our view—demand that the president generally be an accomplished academic, a profession that does not typically involve the managerial or political skills required of a college president.

It is not surprising that many long-lasting university presidents who were not academics were politicians. The most obvious example is Woodrow Wilson, who served as president of Princeton from 1902 to 1910 before becoming president in 1913. Donna Shalala had a successful tenure as chancellor of the University of Wisconsin before serving as the secretary of health and human services; she later returned to academia as the president of the University of Miami. When asked what she did well as a university president, Shalala said, "Making the institution feel better about itself. Increasingly, I've come to believe that it's not the specific agenda that leaders have, but the atmosphere they create on campus so other leaders and other parts of the university really feel freed up and supported in doing the things they've always wanted to do."[8]

Terry Sanford was a highly successful president of Duke University after serving as governor of North Carolina and before returning to politics as a U.S. senator. Mitch Daniels was governor of Indiana from 2005 to 2013 before becoming president of Purdue University, and Margaret Spellings was secretary of education from 2005 to 2009 before becoming president of the University of North Carolina in 2016. It is also notable that Bart Giamatti became the commissioner of baseball, a highly political position, after serving as president of Yale. The skills needed to win elections or run Major League Baseball are similar to those needed to run a university.

THE PRESIDENT MUST SERVE
MULTIPLE STAKEHOLDERS

It is an understatement to say that college presidents work within a complex governance structure. Internally, they must deal with academic superstars, student activists, critical student newspapers, and often athletic departments under great pressure to produce winning teams, to name just a few. At the same time, they must work with a board that hired them in the first place and can fire them at any time.

At private universities, the chancellor reports to the board of trustees. Typically, the board has a chair and an executive committee, and there is a relatively predictable pattern of succession. Although working with such a board is challenging, the private university chancellor plays a role in building the board and can therefore predict with some accuracy its future composition.

For public university chancellors, the environment is more complex. A few, such as the University of Michigan, have a single board that is similar to those at private schools, but many public universities are part of university systems that are governed by a system president or chancellor.[9] This means that the system president has a line of authority that runs parallel to that of the campus board. In some systems, there is a system board as well, placing the chancellor in the position of working for a campus board, a system board, and a system president.

Government regulations, such as open meeting laws requiring that any communication involving more than a few board members be open to the public, severely restrict the informal communication that good leadership typically requires. Public university leaders often must convene multiple telephone calls discussing the same issues with individual trustees because involving the entire board on the phone at one time requires an open meeting. More fundamentally, the goals of the university system are often at odds with those of the individual campuses. This is often the case when it comes to the state's flagship campuses, which measure success against national and international criteria that could be quite different from the priorities of other system schools.

To add to the complexity, all public university chancellors directly or indirectly serve their state legislatures. Public universities receive significant support from state appropriations that depend on the votes of legislators, and the schools are typically subject to the state personnel system and other regulations of state government. State money typically comes with extensive legislative scrutiny of university expenditures. Even though the bigger public universities often receive significant support from private sources and the federal government, the media and the public generally regard all of the university's budget as public money subject to public scrutiny. True to its mission to "comfort the afflicted and afflict the comfortable," the press is quick to pursue questions of how much something cost and who paid for it.

UNC–Chapel Hill chancellor Carol Folt told us how interacting with people outside the academy contributed to her ideas of how to lead a public university. "I started appreciating that people didn't understand [the] research [that the university did] but were proud of it," she said. "I started appreciating how business people talked about it." She said that the more she talked to folks outside the academy, the more interesting and different questions she heard. "Everyone I ever worked with said they loved the university," but their perspectives were very different from those of professors or reviewers on a National Institutes of Health panel. "They would ask you about operations, why things didn't make sense, what were we thinking when we made those decisions. Those were really helpful, and when [matters turned] financial, I started really understanding what people were worried about and why."

THE ROLE OF TRUSTEE IS COMPLICATED

In a complex system based on consensus, trustees provide necessary oversight. When we asked Washington University trustee Gene Kahn how long it took him to understand the workings of the university, he said,

"I hope I live that long." Learning those nuances is difficult, takes a great deal of time, and is "very experiential learning; it's not practical learning." Kahn feels that his primary obligations are "to assure that I'm a good financial steward of the university, to ensure our efforts to accomplish our strategic initiatives and evolve to a place where we are never resting or happy where we are, and to attract at the undergraduate and graduate level the best, the brightest, and the most diverse."

It may be possible to design a governing body more complicated than the board of a college or university, but we doubt it. Generally, they are too big, too political, and too removed from the realities of the institutions they represent. Yet, in the words of President Gordon Gee, the presence of a lay board is a requirement for the university to do its job. The board bridges the gap between the ivory tower and the rest of the world and also represents the various external constituencies with an interest in the university. Since both public and private schools receive direct and indirect government subsidies—direct at state universities and less direct at privates, through federal research, financial aid support, and the tax exemption—lay governance to oversee this enormous public investment is essential.

Nothing we say here about the inherent complexities is meant to downplay the importance of and need for lay governance. Simply put, university trustees are on the firing line as the critical issues facing higher education are renegotiated. They, along with the chancellor, are direct representatives of the public interests outside the walls of the university, just as the chancellor and administration represent the interests inside the walls. The chancellor is expected to live in both worlds.

The selection of trustees is very different in public and private universities. In private universities, generally a nominating committee proposes new trustees, and in most cases the chancellor is a member of the nominating committee, guaranteeing a connection between internal leadership and the external governing body. Trusteeship at private universities often comes as a result of a large gift to the institution, and it is possible for large donors to stay on the board for long periods of time, even for life. As a result, boards can often be too big to effectively engage or manage, and there is typically an executive committee that meets more frequently.

Selection at public universities is even more involved. Public university trustees are typically appointed by politicians, often in exchange for campaign support and political fundraising. The chancellor has almost no role in selecting these trustees and often first meets new trustees after they are appointed. Trustees are usually term-limited, so they only have a short time horizon in which to learn the ropes and make a contribution. Indeed, search consultants have told us they can often tell when a presidency is about to end because trustees' terms are running out and they want to be part of picking the new president.

Although the responsibilities of trustees are almost always clearly stated in the governing documents of a university, the reality is often different. As the Sullivan case demonstrates, although the board clearly holds the responsibility for hiring and assessing the chancellor, the board cannot ignore internal constituencies, such as faculty and students, or external forces, such as alumni, governmental officials, and the public at large. In the current landscape of higher education it is not difficult to find other examples of key hiring decisions gone wrong when a board failed to gain consensus while making a high-profile appointment.[10]

The board almost always has formal authority over the investments of the institution, typically delegated to a committee of members who are experienced investors, but they likely will not have had experience with movements to convince institutions to divest themselves of holdings in Sudan, fossil fuels, and other issues to come.[11] A shift at the Ford Foundation toward "impact investing" for a portion of its endowment will inevitably increase the interest of students and faculty in the way the university's endowments are being invested.[12] Moreover, federal and state policy may impact the board's authority by prescribing how much of an endowment must be allocated to financial aid.[13]

Often, the board is less constrained in exercising its authority over the physical appearance of the campus. Typically, they establish buildings and grounds committees that oversee the selection of architects, the design of new buildings, decisions about changing the layout of the campus, and the acquisition of nearby real estate. Interestingly, this is an area boards often feel strongly about, taking seriously how the public feels about the appearance of the campus. Even here, outside constituencies often intervene, as evidenced by the movements in campus communities to rename buildings and to make them environmentally sustainable.[14] Large donors often have understandably strong feelings as well about the architecture of buildings named for them.

Trustees also have a formal role in matters related to internal audits and potential legal actions that challenge the university. Increasingly, other constituencies have become interested in the finances of colleges and universities, and this places greater stress on financial controls that were formerly opaque and are now quite transparent. Regarding legal action, the board usually makes the decision whether to defend university employees from increasingly common lawsuits. Although the decision is almost always to defend the employees who were acting in their official capacity, the role of the board in these decisions is quite important.

Fundraising is another vital board function. Trustees are often major donors, and the board usually has a development committee that is responsible for planning and executing fundraising campaigns. Faculty and students are typically content to leave this activity to the trustees, but successful campaigns necessitate deep involvement by the entire community and require clear plans for involving key faculty and impressive students to become partners in engaging major donors.

When we asked Carol Folt how trustees at a public university can be of most help, she—like many other chancellors—said that they need to focus on strategy and not operations. She stressed that the most helpful trustees are ones who "feel like [they] can ask questions, because it's [their] questions about what we do that help us understand how to be clear to everybody." Folt believes that trustees are the best bridge to citizens who are disconnected from the university. "I need [their] help," she says, "in making sure that the people who feel disenfranchised from Carolina have a voice—and [they] open the conduit."

Most of the important decisions that happen at universities do not require board approval, but a well-functioning board can make important contributions. For example, a well-functioning board will delegate authority to the president to pick an administrative team; a lack of trust in the president to name this team is typically a sign of trouble. It is a good practice, though, to include one or more trustees on the search committees for important officers, and smart presidents keep trustees engaged as the process moves forward. In the words of Gordon Gee, university leaders should "pick up the damn telephone." When the appointment of important deans or vice chancellors are advancing, smart presidents are working the phones. MIT trustee Desh Deshpande told us that the board should hire the president and the president should be charged with other personnel decisions, but the board can suggest best practices and push to make sure the hiring processes identify the best people.

The next area where informal board communication is critical relates to matters that appear in the media. No board member wants to be surprised by a question from an acquaintance about something in the newspaper. When that happens, the trustee is embarrassed not to have known about the matter or to have a response. Anticipating issues in advance and talking them through with experienced trustees will invariably result in a better response, and the process will help build support on the board for the president as he or she articulates the agreed-upon position.

Inevitably, trustees want to be involved in matters of undergraduate education, and it is important to keep them up to speed on the issues surrounding the campus experience. Trustees are anxious to weigh in, based on their experiences in college. This can be a complication, and it is often said that trustees (and alumni) remember the university the way it never was. Considerable artistry can be required to leverage the trustees' natural interest in the student experience without giving them undue influence over an environment that is quite different from the one they remember. (Such focus typically does not extend to graduate education and research because few with graduate student experience serve as trustees. In fact, engaging the interest of trustees in research and graduate education is a major challenge at research universities.)

Former MIT chancellor Phillip Clay believes that this informal communication can best achieved by using board members as "informal advisers." In his view, involving the board in ongoing, off-the-record conversations is a way to address the need to keep them informed and to receive valuable advice not typically available from inside academia. However, for this to work, "they have to know what's going on."

One of the most delicate and difficult tasks is to help the board understand the idea of shared governance and the parts of the university where they have almost no control, and—even more challenging—where their intervention will inhibit their desired outcome. This is perhaps most apparent in the areas where faculty have almost complete autonomy: graduate admissions, the granting of tenure, the recruiting of new tenure-track colleagues, curricula, and advising the administration on academic freedom. Again, the University of Virginia experience is instructive: trustees attempted to intervene in matters of curriculum in response to the feverish excitement over online education. Board members from the corporate world are used to moving fast in response to short-term economic developments, but the faculty and their colleagues around the country firmly resisted this infringement on faculty authority.

Another common area of board confusion is faculty appointments. The board is often involved in raising money for new research centers; if the leader of the new research institute is to be a tenured faculty member, however, the trustees have little or no say as to who will fill that appointment. This is counterintuitive to people from the corporate world—if they give a big gift to the university, why can't they be involved in selecting the person to lead the new entity? Or if they help attract a big gift to create a new academic program, why should they have to go through faculty committees to determine whether the program can be offered at the university and what the content should be?

This separation of responsibilities—part of shared governance—is vital to maintaining what is great about American higher education. The trick for chancellors and presidents is to keep all parties focused on their own responsibilities while understanding and respecting the larger system that they serve and their contributions to its betterment and sustainability.

EFFECTIVE LEADERSHIP TAKES A VARIETY OF FORMS

Gordon Gee, who has been a college president for thirty-five years in seven assignments and Mark Wrighton, who has served for twenty-two years as the chancellor of Washington University in St. Louis, illustrate two distinct approaches to leading a college or university. Gee's list of accomplishments includes heading a $2.5 billion fundraising campaign with $100 million dedicated to need-based, in-state scholarships while at Ohio State; radically restructuring athletics at Vanderbilt; and dramatically reversing declines in enrollment while increasing the quality of incoming classes at West Virginia.[15]

Wrighton is also a prodigious fundraiser, having raised more than $3 billion for Washington University in one campaign alone. He also presided over the construction of fifty new buildings and the creation of 165 endowed professorships. Most recently, he engineered a dramatic improvement in the diversity of the Washington University student body by raising more than $500 million for financial aid.[16]

Gordon Gee—Change Agent

Gordon Gee was first appointed president at West Virginia University in 1981 at the age of thirty-seven. Since then, he has served as president at the University of Colorado, Ohio State University, Brown University, Vanderbilt University, Ohio State (a second time), and West Virginia (a second time). It is unlikely that his career will ever be duplicated. No stranger to controversy, Gee has made many of these moves during periods of turmoil, but he always emerges at another great school and he always makes an enormous impact.

Gee's style is to be transparent in difficult situations. This transparency sometimes creates controversy, but it can also be endearing, at least to his admirers. When Ohio State's championship coach Jim Tressel was accused of violating ethics rules, the media asked Gee if he was going to fire him. "Are you kidding?" he said. "I'm just hopeful the coach doesn't dismiss me." Although this statement probably didn't help Gee's situation at Ohio State, many of his colleagues around the country who struggled with big-time sports received it with knowing appreciation.

A subsequent sequence of leaked comments about Ohio State football, in which Gee joked about not playing "the Little Sisters of the Poor" and the academic reputation of the University of Louisville, led to his departure, and his next planned stop was a teaching position at Harvard. Predictably, he was called home to West Virginia to be interim president, and to the surprise of no one, he was soon named the permanent president of WVU.

Gee is quite forthcoming about his unconventional career.

> I was thirty-six when I became a university president, so I was the youngest president in the country for a long period of time. . . . I have always been outspoken and active. . . . What happens is . . . you wear out your welcome and you also wear out your freshness, and . . . universities are like anything else. They need to constantly refresh themselves and so they need to have new leadership after a period of time—five to seven years. [Also] you need to reinvent yourself, . . . and in my instance because I really enjoyed being a university president, I felt that I needed to really be challenged again. If you do one of these jobs too long, you start feeling like you are running a marathon around the block. You started seeing the same things over and over again and it becomes a habit rather than an exciting opportunity, and so you constantly have to reinvent yourself. Now you can do that in place, there is no doubt about it, and I know some of our colleagues have done that in place, but for me it was the opportunity of making myself better and refreshing myself and reenergizing myself.

About returning to West Virginia University, he says, "I tell everyone that I came back to undo all the mistakes I made the first time around." After he characterized an administrative practice as the "dumbest damn thing I have ever seen in my life," the retort was, "Yes, you created that while you were here the first time."

Despite tangles with his boards, Gee is a strong believer in lay leadership for universities. In a wide-ranging talk that he gave to the Southern University Conference in 2016, Gee laid out several practices needed for successful board leadership of universities. In his typical wry style, he points out that in a survey of college presidents about their boards, the two biggest problems were "lack of engagement" and "micromanagement." "In truth," he says, "most presidents see the value in governing boards whose members are living links to the world beyond the ivory tower."

"Negotiating the delicate balance between president and board—between management and governance—is a skill that must be learned," he goes on to say. "Mostly it is learned through trial and error because no one takes a college class on this stuff." Regarding President Clark Kerr of the University of California who, despite revolutionizing our ideas of a public university, was "fired with enthusiasm" by the regents, Gee says, "I have exceeded his tenure as a president by more than two decades and have never been 'fired with enthusiasm,' although I have occasionally been bid farewell with great sighs of relief."

In a point that illustrates the sorts of misconceptions that led to the events at the University of Virginia, Gee says, "While it is important to keep your board happy, it is more important to meet the needs of your constituents—faculty, staff, alumni, and especially students. It is vital because these are the people who make your institution what it is. As a side benefit, if your board becomes unhappy with you, good relationships with these groups can save you—at least for a while."

Gee demonstrates how a relatively short tenure as a college president can still make an enormous impact. And his career offers another important lesson: despite his stirring up controversy wherever he goes, another school has always wanted his talents. That is due to his enormous energy and sense of humor, and because few individuals in his line of work have his experience (including the battle scars) and ability to get things done in the academic environment.

Mark Wrighton—Playing the Long Game

It would be difficult to find a greater contrast to Gee than Mark Wrighton, the long-serving chancellor of Washington University. Wrighton was a wunderkind of science in his early career, when he flew through graduate school in a little more than two years and became a tenure-track professor at MIT at the age of twenty-three and a full professor at twenty-eight. In 1983, he received a MacArthur "genius" grant. During his research career, he published more than three hundred papers and was cited over twenty-five thousand times. He became the chair of MIT's chemistry department at age thirty-eight and provost of the university three years later.

In 1995, Washington University was surging into the ranks of elite private universities thanks to the leadership of its chancellor, William Danforth. It was home to a top medical school, and the undergraduate program was gaining in prominence. When Danforth announced his retirement, the university turned to Wrighton, who brought the same energy that propelled his academic career to his role as chancellor of the university.

In contrast to Gee, Wrighton steers away from controversy. The closest he came to the controversies Gee has experienced was his board's decision to give an honorary degree to right-wing firebrand Phyllis Schlafly. Wrighton deftly upheld the decision of the board while stating his personal objections to Schlafly's ideas. This approach to keeping the waters calm over many years has allowed Wrighton to dramatically influence the direction of the university.

When Wrighton moved to Washington University, some questioned why he moved to St. Louis when, as MIT provost, he could have held out for an Ivy League job. "I'll tell you what I was thinking about interviewing for the job," he said. "I said to myself there are twenty places that are private major-league research institutions and the presidents and chancellors stay about ten years, and there are two places therefore per year that are going to have an opening. So when this opportunity came, I thought, this looks interesting, high quality. And it's better than I thought it would be."

Wrighton is an admirer of Gordon Gee, who he says is a "remarkable person"; being rehired by two places he left strikes Wrighton as "extraordinary." Still, Wrighton volunteers quickly that the Gee path is not something he could do. He says he went to Washington University thinking he would stay eight to ten years and then move on to a job running a museum or foundation. As the inevitable offers came in, however, he never saw anything that made him want to stop doing what he was doing in St. Louis.

Continuity has been incredibly helpful to Wrighton in fundraising. He has led two successful campaigns. "It takes a long time," he says. "Fundraising is a very important part of these jobs, and what you have to invest in is finding out what people would be interested in, getting to understand that interest, and somehow making the case that if they give you money, you can help them fulfill their interest. Many people mistake that fundraising is identifying a person who has capacity and then you ask them for a gift, and that's part of it, but that comes far down the road." Wrighton's patience and longevity are a huge help. Wrighton took his dogged obsession with chemistry and traded it for the same level of commitment and curiosity about people, a trait that turns out to be Wrighton's high card.

When we asked Gee how he kept fresh, he said that he had to reinvent himself and for him that meant changing universities. Wrighton has a different perspective:

> When I was active as a research faculty member, I did not like to give the same talk twice even if it meant I would only change the order of the presentation. But I've come to appreciate that one of the most important things to do in this role is—as we represent the university— to be consistent in the communication, so that when people network with each other they can say things like, did you hear Mark Wrighton talk about the importance of genetics and genomics at Washington University? I think you have to be responsive to the audience, but the core messages need to remain the same, and when I'm reminded of the great things that can come from our research, it excites me to have people show interest in what our faculty and students are doing. That's kind of the reward. Most people who know me know that I don't speak from a prepared text. It's dangerous in this world to do that. But I think it's better to try to speak extemporaneously, and I use few visuals.

Few college presidents will serve in seven posts; neither will many serve in a single job for more than twenty-two years. But what both Gee and Wrighton have in common—and what all effective presidents must surely strive for—is a deep understanding of the importance of the relationships they must maintain with their various constituencies.

LEADERSHIP HAS NEVER BEEN MORE IMPORTANT

The dynamics facing leaders of universities—presidents and boards—would be challenging in any environment. The accumulation of relationships and political capital, the decisions about when to expend what you have accumulated, and the adroit interaction with constituencies are no easy assignments. As our profiles of Gee and Wrighton illustrate, this is an art rather than a science and must be learned through experience.

Today's leaders—and we include both administration and board members in this category—face greater challenges today than ever before. As we have discussed, the pressures from demographics, arithmetic, and technology require bold decision-making. Leadership needs to engage in cold analysis of the forces facing an institution, and then in the more challenging task of implementing change. This will require even greater attention to the accumulation of political capital and the cultivation of relationships. To that end, the board must understand that the president needs help in securing the support of internal constituencies, and to achieve that support, some board actions may need to be delayed or deflected in order to preserve the necessary level of consensus.

At the beginning of this chapter, we discussed a bold board decision that went badly awry, and we have also seen what happened at Sweet Briar College and others. In contrast, the patient and persistent leadership of Michael Crow at Arizona State and Marty Meehan at the University of Massachusetts–Lowell show that boldness is possible even within the university governance matrix. But to be effective, both administrators and board members must rise above episodic and often manufactured crises such as the University of Virginia incident and focus on the future. Part of what is needed is experience—administrators struggle with matters that they are facing for the first time but can better focus on the big picture when the episode of the day is one they have seen before.

How can boards help? Remember our long-serving trustee who hoped to live long enough to understand the workings of the university? Most trustees are engaged because of the strong feelings they have for their undergraduate experience, and this will always be an area of focus. But the research, financial, legal, medical, and operations areas of the university are complex and in need of board attention. Trustees should resist the urge to focus on their own experiences and should try to understand the complexities of other areas of the university.

If you are a trustee and you have read this far, then you are trying. When Holden was chancellor, one trustee told him, "I never thought about the fact that you were running an airport, a hotel, and a police department." A shared understanding of the whole institution can alleviate the gridlock that sometimes sets in during a crisis. Finally, when the president doesn't want to take an action because of how it will play with faculty or students, stop and think about whether the costs of pushing that action are worth it.

What can chancellors do? As Gee says, accept that lay leadership of universities is a requirement and can be a positive factor, recognize that, paradoxically, "lack of engagement" and "micromanagement" will somehow coexist, and work hard to get everyone to understand the issues. Gee also says that when there is a problem, "put the skunk on the table."[17] It's best to "pick up the telephone and talk about problems before they become a crisis." Resist the urge to do everything the board asks before contemplating whether it will cause political problems with other constituencies. Also, slow down: most leaders got where they are by doing tasks quickly and well; executive leadership requires more contemplation. Wrighton frequently says, "I need to sleep on it." He sleeps on things because he needs to think through how decisions will play through the rest of the organization.

All of this hard work is badly needed as the struggle continues to rebuild trust with those interested in the future of American higher education. The multifaceted problems we have discussed thus far can be solved only when the parties are in open and transparent dialogue. Gee told us that those within the university sometimes have a limited view. They "believe that we are for the university or we are for research or we are for something else, but we don't have wider responsibilities." Rather, Gee says, both public and private institutions need to reestablish the compact that public education, public higher education, is for the public good. As he said, "We are not simply here to teach or to discover or to write the great American novel or to find the cure for cancer. Those are important but it does us no good if the people in McDowell County in southern West Virginia aren't helped, if they don't have the access to this. So that's the compact that we need to reestablish."

Academic Medicine—
The Elephant in the Room

Talking about higher education without talking about academic medicine is like talking about the federal government without talking about Medicare and Social Security. Ironically, discussion of academic medicine tends to be a once-a-year event in the work of the board of trustees, and every trustee we interviewed told us that the board doesn't know enough about the medical enterprise. "When you think of the amount of influence the medical school has both on the amount of people it educates and the amount of service it gives back," said Washington University trustee Gene Kahn, "the board spends less time on it than it could or maybe should." Campus tours rarely route through the academic hospital, and the towering medical buildings are often at architectural odds with the idyllic quads and ivy-covered buildings of the academic campus. Nonetheless, when influential donors need to see one of the university's world-class specialists, the first call they make is to the chancellor to arrange an appointment. Though not the most glamorous subject, academic medicine will be central to the conversation surrounding higher education's responsibility to the public, and all involved avoid its intricacies at their peril.

THE WAR ON DISEASE

Only 147 universities in the United States have medical schools, but nearly every college and university supplies talent and ideas to the American medical system. In making the argument for the birth of federally funded science, Vannevar Bush led with what has always been the high card: the war on disease. No aspect of the discovery enterprise has the political power and influence of biomedical research. Research funded by the National Institutes of Health generates about $60 billion in economic activity annually;[1] the 1,038 teaching hospitals in the United States treat 18 million admitted patients and handle 291 million outpatient visits;[2] graduate medical education represents $15 billion of the federal budget;[3] and the prestige of working at a great American academic medical center is a powerful draw for the best researchers and clinicians from all over the world.

The enterprise that has resulted from the combination of high-performance clinical care and pioneering science is a stunning success story. Academic medicine has given birth to large university-based health care systems such as Partners HealthCare and Harvard University in Boston,[4] BJC Healthcare and Washington University in St. Louis,[5] and the University of Pittsburgh Medical Center (UPMC) and the University of Pittsburgh.[6] Health care systems associated with top medical schools employ world-class physicians at below-market compensation because these physicians want to work at world-class medical centers and because they get protected time away from the clinic for research. Patients seek out these medical centers because the imprimatur of the university both implies and delivers a higher standard of care and access to new, cutting-edge cures. Depending on the insurance environment and competition, these juggernauts can sometimes command a premium on reimbursements, delivering the most profitable care. As a result, academic medical centers have become dominant economic forces in their regions: BJC is the largest employer in Missouri, and UPMC is the largest nongovernmental employer in Pennsylvania.[7]

Despite the enormous scientific and economic impact of these organizations, university stakeholders are not adequately informed about or engaged in their operations. Trustees are often more comfortable focusing on the things they know best—the undergraduate experience and athletics—and seldom devote significant time to academic medicine, even though the greater part of the risk, opportunity, and budget associated with the university is located in the university hospital and not in the football stadium or the student union. The war on disease is still the strongest calling card the university has. If we are to renegotiate the partnership with the public, academic medicine along with research and teaching in health-related fields must be recognized as primary obligations on the part of higher education. We realize that not all institutions have medical schools, but one way or another academic medicine will affect virtually every college and university and the people they serve.[8]

The medical school can also be the source of great angst for university presidents. "Docs and jocks" are often cited as the biggest thorns in the sides of leaders, and—as we will detail below—the medical school can create a great deal of leadership tension. In an old joke, a university president dies and thinks he has gone to hell but is pleasantly surprised to find that he has plenty of money and a beautiful office. When he asks his assistant if he is in heaven, the assistant replies, "No sir, you have two medical schools." We cannot overstate the importance to all stakeholders of understanding the complexities associated with academic medicine.

THE RELATIONSHIP BETWEEN THE HOSPITAL AND THE MEDICAL SCHOOL IS CRITICAL

It is often said, "If you've seen one academic medical center, you've seen one academic medical center." No two are alike, and relationships among the chancellor, board, medical school dean, health care system CEO, trustees, health care system board members, and provost can vary enormously from school to school. Nonetheless, some commonalities can be applied across the board so long as leadership understands both worlds. A degree of mistrust typically inheres in the relationship. As Kahn told us, "Both trustees of Washington University, who don't have a lot of practical experience with the medical school, and [hospital] trustees, who don't have a lot of experience with Washington University, are very suspect of the genuineness of the relationship."

There are important distinctions between the two institutions that need to be understood. First, there is an important difference between the teaching hospital and the medical school. Typically, the medical school—led by an academic dean who usually has an academic background—is responsible for the medical school faculty, who are both researchers and clinicians, and the medical students, who include students in the M.D. programs, Ph.D. programs in biomedicine, and allied health programs such as audiology or physical therapy. The teaching hospital—led usually by a hospital CEO and sometimes its own board—is the place where the faculty provide clinical care, train medical students and residents, and conduct clinical trials related to their research. In some systems, the dean of the medical school is also the CEO of the hospital, while in others, the primary teaching hospital may be part of a larger system of hospitals in the region.

Another important difference is the faculty practice plan, which is generally the organization that employs the faculty physicians and compensates them for their time in the clinic. The hospital and faculty practice can reside inside or outside of the university. Commonly the faculty practice plan is part of the university, and faculty compensation is internally determined based on time spent in the medical school or the practice plan. At a few institutions the faculty practice plan exists outside of the university. The most notable example is the University of Pittsburgh, where medical school faculty get two paychecks—one from the medical school and one from the faculty practice plan, which is located in UPMC and not in the university.

It is also common for the hospital to exist separately from the university. The University of Pittsburgh Medical Center and BJC Healthcare are separate organizations, although university administrators serve on the boards. At Harvard, the hospitals are so separate that the research grants flow to the four teaching hospitals—Massachusetts General, Brigham and Women's, Boston Children's, and Beth Israel—and not to the medical school. The hospitals even have their own technology transfer operations to commercialize the inventions of the faculty. In contrast, at the University of Michigan, the CEO of the health care system reports to the president of the university. At a few places, such as Case Western Reserve, the hospital is very distant from the medical school.

In whatever form, the interaction between the university and the medical center is important, because the clinical profits of the hospital are a significant source of revenue for the medical school—though the amount and process can vary enormously. At some institutions, a predetermined fraction of the hospital profit goes back to the medical school; at others, the medical school has to ask the health care system for transfers throughout the year. These transfers are usually referred to as "funds flow," and the nature of this subsidy and how the transfers are handled are absolutely critical to the success of the medical school.

Within the hospital and practice plan, cross-subsidy among specialties is common. Typically, only a few parts of the clinical effort are profitable—cardiology, oncology, and the procedural specialties, such as surgery, orthopedics, and neurosurgery. Some of the clinical departments, particularly neurology and psychiatry, operate at steep deficits. The largest department is the department of medicine (which creates confusion with the *school* of medicine), which typically includes infectious disease, gastroenterology, cardiology, oncology, and endocrinology. The medical school is not sustainable unless the profitable specialties subsidize the others. This is why the nature of the funds flow is so important. The result is that academic medical centers are sometimes the only places where patients can get high-quality psychiatric or neurological care.

EXTERNALLY FUNDED MEDICAL RESEARCH IS A DRAIN ON A UNIVERSITY'S BUDGET

At first glance, the biomedical research undertaken in the medical school appears to be a moneymaker for the university. The university is always touting its ranking and success in garnering research grants, mostly from the federal government but also from industry and foundations. Federal research grants come with "indirect costs," additional monies provided to the university to subsidize the administrative costs that attend the execution of the funded research.

Typically, the federal government gives the university an additional forty cents for every dollar of funded research. The public perceives all of this as profit to the university. Shockingly, a sober accounting of the true costs demonstrates that there is no greater drain on the university budget than externally funded research.[9] This is because the additional costs of carrying out the research are not adequately funded by the indirect cost rate.

The investments required to conduct federal research are important. "When I tell our board that we're having to put more than twenty-five cents on every dollar into the research enterprise because the sponsors won't pay the full cost," says Mark Wrighton, "some board members say, well why don't you get out of that business? My response is that *is* our business and we can't get out of it."

The costs of carrying out funded research are extensive. Most funded research occurs in laboratories that are expensive to build and maintain. Administering research grants involves complying with extensive federal regulations, which have grown in complexity without a corresponding growth in indirect cost reimbursement. New researchers generate few grants at the beginning of their careers, necessitating a start-up package that provides funds to set up a laboratory and pay for research for the period before the new professor gets his or her first grant. When academic researchers are wooed by other universities, they are often offered additional packages to subsidize their research, as an inducement to stay. New graduate students usually are not paid for on grants at the beginning of their education; the university generally bears this cost. Further, clinicians who produce enormous clinical revenue often bargain for laboratories for research even though their laboratories do not receive outside funding. In such cases the university subsidizes the clinicians' research in order to retain their substantial clinical revenues.

Owing to all these indirect costs, the university becomes a significant funder of biomedical research. The Association of American Medical Colleges (AAMC) estimates that academic medical centers provide fifty-three cents of additional funding for every dollar of outside research funding.[10] Exacerbating this problem, funding from foundations, including such large funders as the Gates Foundation, do not provide significant subsidies for indirect costs. The implications of this indirect cost shortfall are enormous.

The first is the drain on the university budget. As Chris Newfield detailed in his book on public universities, *The Great Mistake*, the funds used to subsidize research often come from core activities of the university that do not generate outside revenue.[11] On the academic affairs side of the university, this means that English literature can end up paying for chemistry and biology. Within the medical school, it means that the money-losing specialties have less subsidy to rely on. At most places that have profitable specialties, the biomedicine enterprise does not drain the academic affairs portion of the university directly, although the situation limits the possibility that the profitable medical school specialties could significantly subsidize academic affairs.

The second implication is that the university is a large funder of biomedical research but generally has no cogent strategy or philosophy as to how that money is spent. The allocation of the internal subsidy is largely ad hoc: the funds are used to start careers, sustain clinical profits, and fill in gaps. Occasionally, a medical school will collect clinical profits and apply them to a specific goal such as bioinformatics or personalized medicine, but this is done with great difficulty, as the individual departments and programs fight to claim subsidies or protect the profits that they generate.

There is a great opportunity in American academic medicine for the individual schools and the collective group of AAMC members to adopt a better strategic focus for their contributions to biomedical research. After the National Institutes of Health, the AAMC schools themselves are the largest funders of biomedical research in the country—even larger than the pharmaceutical industry. If this horsepower could be directed in a compelling way, it could contribute significantly to the renewal of the partnership that we are recommending.[12]

TRANSLATIONAL MEDICINE IS EXPECTED

More than in any other area of the university, the public expects the research done in the academic medical center to produce innovations that improve human health and produce better outcomes for patients. This is a double-edged sword: on the one hand, the public is more accepting and supportive of medical research than of other university research initiatives; on the other, the expectations for breakthroughs are higher and more urgent. In truth, most of the research done in the university is closer to basic science, so administrators and the funding agencies are always pushing for more translational research that takes basic science from the bench to the bedside. Some of this translational research can result in licensed technology that will eventually benefit the public. Some may involve running clinical trials or other clinical studies that produce new practice interventions; this latter area is usually referred to as implementation science.

Talking about this area with stakeholders or the public requires balancing the great potential for medical breakthroughs against the time and uncertainty of realizing them. Many scientific breakthroughs, such as the discovery of monoclonal antibodies or the sequencing of the human genome, took years or even decades to reach the bedside. So even though chancellors and medical school deans feel enormous pressure to tout potential breakthroughs to alumni and politicians, they need to guard against overpromising. Further, most academic medical centers have attractive hooks tailor-made for conversations with the public (for example, cancer immunology, the microbiome, and Alzheimer's disease), but overemphasizing these areas in the public discourse runs the risk of alienating other researchers at the university. In the end, most leaders decide to highlight the strengths and manage the grumbling from other quarters that feel—usually for good reasons—that they deserve more attention.

ACADEMIC MEDICINE IS A
HUGE ECONOMIC ENGINE

The presence of a university in a town or city can be an enormous economic boon, and no university function drives a regional economy like academic medicine. The continued growth of health care as a proportion of gross domestic product (GDP) plus the large investments in research provide an engine of economic activity that dwarfs any other function the university can mount. This is why some of the most challenging politics in higher education leadership revolve around the ownership and location of medical schools.

The launch of the East Carolina School of Medicine in North Carolina, for example, created a political firestorm that defined the long tenure of William Friday as the legendary first president of the UNC system.[13] And in the Salaita case at the University of Illinois discussed in chapter 5, it was revealed in emails released later that a backdrop of the controversy was the desire by the Champaign campus to preserve political capital needed to launch a medical school in the face of resistance from the campus in Chicago.[14]

The difficult politics associated with academic medicine are worth the fight, however. When the enterprise is going strong, it can be a source of both economic and political strength. The jobs and construction that the effort brings provide an enormous presence. Indeed, the recent evolution of many U.S. cities is centered in the academic medicine enterprise. Minneapolis, Pittsburgh, and St. Louis were once dominated respectively by the Fortune 500 industries 3M, PPG, and McDonnell-Douglas. Now these cities are largely defined by their universities and their health care centers.

"Meds and Eds" are now coveted by all great American cities.[15] Some have contemplated how Detroit might have evolved if the University of Michigan were in Detroit and not an hour away in Ann Arbor.[16] Beyond the economic activity, the goodwill generated by these enterprises is also extremely important. Grateful patients, start-up activity of associated companies, and groundbreaking medical research provide the university with friends and stories that build political capital. All of this reinforces Vannevar Bush's logic that the war on disease was the most effective political argument for federal research funding.

ACADEMIC MEDICINE PRESENTS UNIQUE CHALLENGES AND OPPORTUNITIES

University leadership must manage the campus politics that result from the presence of a medical school with great care. Jim Duderstadt, the long-serving and highly successful president of the University of Michigan, famously said, "The great challenge of the Michigan presidency is to protect the fragile character of the university's academic programs from being overwhelmed or pulled asunder by the ever-present distraction and threat of the Athletic Department on one end of campus and the Medical Center on the other."[17]

The disciplines that do not feel the luster of the academic medicine enterprise naturally feel left out, and as Chris Newfield has detailed, the necessity to subsidize research can have an adverse effect on the budgets of the nonmedical disciplines.[18] Further, it is healthiest for the university if the academic affairs side of the university is generating external grants at a rate similar to that of the medical school. Schools such as the universities of Michigan, Washington, and North Carolina rank high on the list of schools receiving federal funding because they have grants outside of the medical school that are comparable to their substantial medical funding.[19] Other schools whose funding is dominated by the medical school, such as Vanderbilt, Duke, Emory, and Washington University in St. Louis, have to carefully manage morale and resources outside the medical school.

Ultimately, the university community has to work together to ensure that all disciplines benefit from the juggernaut of academic medicine.[20] Achieving this balance is a day-to-day struggle that requires trust and personal capital. It is important for top university leadership to engage deeply with academic medicine *and* to put the thumb on the scale for the other disciplines whenever possible. The engagement with the academic medicine enterprise provides support and builds the trust that is needed to make sure that the effort helps the entire university.

Last, chancellors, provosts, and boards need to wade into the complexity of health care and the economics of research to maintain a presence in the medical enterprise. The financial risks associated with the health care operation are significant: although the dynamics at work today are generally favorable, prudent administrators will acknowledge that the patterns in reimbursement could shift in the future and create large economic problems. Hospital administrators are quick to proclaim with every political shift that there will be economic strain on the hospital and lower levels of subsidy to the medical school. In reality, these changes have generally come more slowly than predicted, as the political mandates are often challenging to implement while the demand for world-class medicine at academic medical centers remains high. By walking the halls and doing a deep dive into the numbers and operations, university administrators can make their own assessments of these extremely important dynamics.

{ 8

Economic Development
Is No Longer Optional

In the words of Professor Michael Porter, "The prosperity of regional economies and the health of their colleges and universities are inescapably linked."[1] Approximately seven thousand colleges and universities in the United States employed 4.1 million people in the fall of 2014, and this segment added 1.6 million new jobs between 1989 and 2014.[2] Higher education in the United States also spent $517 billion on salaries, goods, and services during the 2013–14 academic year.[3] Undeniably, higher education in the United States and elsewhere around the world produces new knowledge that leads to economic growth.

The data confirm that colleges and universities of all sizes—even small schools and those that focus on the liberal arts—drive employment, economic growth, and tax revenues in and around the towns and cities in which they are located and beyond. Economic development has gone from a by-product of higher education to a public expectation, but in this time of rapid economic change and the inevitable dislocations it causes, the public expects more. The renewed partnership with the public will require colleges and universities to accelerate and highlight their role as economic engines.

Like every aspect of rebuilding the partnership, making the case for economic impact is not easy. The public is largely unaware of the effect that academia has on their daily lives. The challenge was articulated clearly for us by Jonathan Cole: "We have to work almost at the grassroots to get people to be aware of this even from the point of view of the economic impact of these universities to the discoveries which have changed their lives. Present them shaped and framed in a way that they can understand, and repeat it, so they can internalize it and not listen to it over lunch and forget about it ten minutes later."

In this chapter and the next, we talk about how to realize the benefits of economic development and entrepreneurship to meet public expectations. But to come back to a point we made in the introduction, we do not view these elements as constituting the purpose of the university, which is education and discovering new knowledge. Rather, success at economic development and entrepreneurship provides a means for establishing the credibility and political capital needed to enable the university's core functions.

RESEARCH UNIVERSITIES PRODUCE HIGH-PROFILE RESULTS

The economic impact of large research universities is well documented. A 2015 report found that MIT alumni had created 30,000 active companies, employing 4.6 million people and producing an annual revenue of $1.9 trillion—equivalent to the world's tenth-largest economy.[4] Harvard alumni were responsible for 146,000 companies, 20.4 million jobs, and $3.9 trillion in revenue.[5] Annual revenue from companies founded by Stanford graduates is estimated at $2.7 trillion, with 18,000 California companies generating $1.27 trillion and employing 3 million people.[6] The University of North Carolina, Duke, and North Carolina State—the three schools in North Carolina's Research Triangle Park (RTP)—combine to generate $19.4 billion in revenue.[7] In fact, RTP is generally recognized as one of the major success stories in translating academic research into economic growth.[8] Colleges and universities in Boston have a similar impact, contributing $4.9 billion to the gross city product.[9] In New York City, new Cornell and New York University sites are slated to contribute $33 billion in revenue over the next thirty years, and Columbia's city-campus partnership will create jobs and provide millions in housing and legal assistance to local neighborhoods.[10]

Similar stories can be told for metropolitan areas as diverse as St. Louis, Providence, and San Diego, where major research universities have had a profound impact on the communities that surround them. In fact, it can be argued that the sixty-two research universities that comprise the Association of American Universities are among the most powerful and reliable generators of economic growth in the U.S. economy.[11] Impressively, between the years 2000 and 2014, among sixteen geographic areas where job growth was strong even in the face of a loss of manufacturing, half were home to a major university.[12] "I think there are a lot of universities that are getting to see this," says Cole, "and are beginning to take this as a formal obligation."

SCHOOLS OF ALL SIZES BENEFIT THE REGIONS AROUND THEM

Hiding beneath the well-known economic impact of America's large research universities is the significant role that smaller entrepreneurial colleges and universities play in stimulating economic development in their local regions. Colleges and universities located in small cities or rural areas often have significant economic impact even when they are not classified as Tier 1 research universities.

Many of the universities established under the Morrill Act and subsequent legislation are located outside of metropolitan areas and have maintained a focus on teaching such practical skills as agriculture and engineering alongside a growing research mission. Historically, manufacturing productivity in counties with land grant colleges has risen faster than similar counties without them, and unemployment rates in those counties average 1.2 percent lower than in the United States as a whole.[13] Moreover, their economies bounced back faster following the Great Recession.[14] In Opelika, Alabama (population 28,000), nearby Auburn University helped replace seven thousand lost jobs with fourteen thousand new ones by attracting new-tech industries like one that uses 3-D printing technology to manufacture jet engine parts.[15] In Murray, Kentucky (population 18,000), the loss of toy manufacturer Mattel resulted in a local unemployment rate of 9.3 percent. Nearby Murray State University, which has strong engineering and business programs, served as a catalyst for Pella Windows to move into the empty plant Mattel left behind. Pella was drawn to a location near a university in large part because the company was based in Pella, Iowa (population 10,000), which is home to Central College, a small liberal arts institution that has been a steady source of Pella employees for years. Already Pella has replaced all of the jobs lost by the Mattel move. Moreover, professors at Auburn and Murray State helped lawn mower manufacturer Briggs and Stratton (which has plants near both campuses) to redesign its lowest-cost engine to compete more effectively with products from China.[16]

Not only do colleges and universities directly create jobs in small towns and cities, but they contribute to economic development and increased tax revenue in what one study labeled the "university effect." The analysis, based on data from fifteen thousand universities across seventy-eight countries, concluded that the presence of a new university in a region increases the region's GDP by 0.4 percent and also increases output in neighboring areas.[17] This conclusion is supported by previous work from the Rand Corporation showing that higher education leads to a 7 to 10 percent rise in earnings per additional year of schooling, which results in substantial increases in tax payments.[18]

START-UPS ARE A BIG PART OF THE EQUATION

Traditionally, universities have partnered with large companies on such efforts as sponsored research, joint product development, licensing of technology, company spin-outs, and outright sales of companies started by university faculty. It is also not unusual for one or more large companies to be major supporters of a college or university on strictly a philanthropic basis.

The U.S. economy is changing, however. Early stage companies have been the primary source of job creation in the American economy since the Great Recession.[19] Not only are these companies a major source of growth, but they contribute to economic dynamism by introducing competition and spurring innovation. Over the past three decades, companies that have operated for less than one year have created an average of 1.5 million jobs annually.[20] Moreover, almost all net new jobs created, as well as 20 percent of the gross jobs created, came from new businesses.[21] During the Great Recession, new companies were the only source of positive net employment growth; older firms shed more jobs than they created.[22]

What this means is that universities must engage with the world of start-ups by encouraging and supporting new enterprises to maximize economic impact. This will be challenging because most new enterprises fail, and failure is anathema to most academics. The culture of innovation must accept and *actually celebrate* failure in order for universities to be fully engaged with the most vibrant sector of the economy. It's also important to point out that the focus on start-ups is not limited to such schools as Stanford and MIT; regional public universities commonly spawn innovation parks nearby.

HOW DOES A UNIVERSITY MAXIMIZE ITS ECONOMIC IMPACT?

Our experience over the past decade has yielded a set of best practices that, if thoughtfully implemented, will allow a university to become a driver of practical innovation and the economic development that goes with it. These practices include the following.

Develop a Strategy

For economic development to be integrated successfully into the academic enterprise, it must be part of a larger innovation strategy that has been accepted and articulated by the faculty and administration. As we discussed in chapter 3, the particulars of the strategy will be as different as the institutions themselves. But there is one constant: developing the strategy will be difficult because of the nature of the academic enterprise and its culture of consensus. The pressure for colleges and universities to do more as part of the discussion of rebuilding the partnership, however, may serve as an impetus for strategy development.

Put another way, many universities may not have a choice. Company creation and job creation will become a requirement for an institution to acquire needed economic and political support. University of North Carolina trustee Lowry Caudill says, "We're going to see [more innovative companies] created in North Carolina and [they will] create jobs, create tax base, and it's a way the university can give back to the state of North Carolina."

Although strategies for economic development will vary by school and region and one size certainly doesn't fit all, a good place to start is with the concept of regional clusters—an idea developed by Porter in connection with his work on the geographic concentrations of interconnected entities within a region.[23] For example, universities can develop job training programs that target local residents to fill the large number of nonacademic jobs that support the school's infrastructure. They can also target a portion of their spending to local businesses to stimulate regional economic growth. Strategic use of an institution's real estate assets can result in economic revitalization, especially in urban areas. University-based incubators and accelerators are other approaches that are currently proving their worth in encouraging company creation and the monetization of new knowledge from university labs.[24]

Whatever strategy is developed, it must also incorporate measurable institutional goals for activities such as job creation, company formation, granting patents, and other relevant criteria, as well as encouragement from the administration and faculty, which includes high-profile speakers and celebrations all aimed at making innovation and entrepreneurship part of the lifeblood of the institution.

Streamline Technology Transfer Policies

For jobs and companies to be created and new knowledge commercialized, universities must make it possible for companies to flourish and technology to be moved outside of academia where its potential can be maximized. This requires policies that make commercialization relatively easy and not something that is viewed as the enemy of independent scientific research. Technology transfer offices, the focal point for commercialization on campus, should facilitate the efforts of faculty entrepreneurs and not become a third point in a triangle comprising the inventor, the licensee, and the tech transfer office.

Start-ups require special care. Licensing can be difficult, because the technology is immature and the principals are often inexperienced at negotiating licenses. Moreover, academics often overestimate the potential value of an enterprise, leading to emotional responses and hurt feelings that are costly to the relationship between the university and the inventor. Tech transfer officers typically worry that they might give away the store the one time a university-based invention becomes highly valuable, and they therefore spend an inordinate amount of time negotiating over what typically amounts to a small sum of money.

One approach to this problem is to develop boilerplate licenses for start-ups. The University of North Carolina initiated one such program, called the Carolina Express License.[25] Washington University, Carnegie Mellon University, and the University of California at San Diego have similar programs. The animating idea behind the boilerplate license is the realization that most licensing negotiations produce roughly the same set of terms when all is said and done. If inventors are given the option of agreeing to the standard license already approved and agreed to by many of their colleagues (and one that is perceived as fair to all concerned), they will generally take the deal.

Most universities have resisted boilerplate licenses because technology transfer professionals tend to view them negatively. They say that each technology is different and requires its own license.[26] Our experience does not support this assertion. Most start-up licenses fall in relatively narrow ranges for equity and royalties, depending on the sector, and an effective express license program can address variances by creating different licenses for different sectors. Some technology transfer officers worry that express licensing programs will undermine their authority and purpose; this fear can be calmed with proper communication and by granting the technology transfer office autonomy and authority in the negotiation of licenses to established companies.

Manage Conflicts of Interests—
Do Not Try to Eliminate Them

One foundation of the university, and the reason academics are drawn to work there, is the principle of curiosity-driven research. To ensure that researchers are truly independent, universities construct conflict of interest policies designed to eliminate economic factors that might compromise the objectivity of research. These policies also prohibit inappropriate use of university resources for the benefit of a commercial enterprise. Michael Hooker, the late chancellor at UNC and a powerful believer that economic activity produced political capital, explained conflict of interest policies to a group of scientists as follows: "Your job is to create conflicts, and my job is to manage them."

There are two schools of thought on how best to manage conflicts of interest, and both have been employed to good effect. The first requires a complete separation between the licensee or spin-out company and the research lab that invented the technology. In this model, the invention is patented or otherwise protected, an academic paper is published, and then the technology is licensed or spun out for commercial development with no ongoing relationship between the commercial enterprise and the academic lab.[27] The second approach is based on the premise that science is better if it is informed by ongoing and open relationships with commercial enterprises, with extensive sharing of information where appropriate. This model allows and even encourages an ongoing relationship between the licensee or spin-out and the laboratory where the technology was created.[28] Typically, the university creates a committee of academics to supervise the relationship, and care is taken to ensure that the cost of any resources dedicated to furthering commercial activities is reimbursed.

We favor the second approach because not only does a relationship with private sector make for better science, but it also furthers the creation of an entrepreneurial culture within the academy, which is so important to the high-impact innovation now required of the academic enterprise.[29]

Bridge the Chasm between the Academy
and Commercialization

It is generally acknowledged that without help, academic research will not easily move from the bench to the market. Until recent years this was not a problem, but the current expectation that academic institutions will be job and company creators requires universities to actively facilitate the commercialization of their research.

Several approaches have had positive outcomes. One of the earliest initiatives, and one that continues to produce results, is the Deshpande Center at MIT. The center catalyzes promising technology by providing ignition grants of $50,000 and, in some cases, awards additional funds up to $250,000. The program also provides a mentor and other business expertise to help companies over what the center refers to as "the valley of death." The Deshpande Center has provided over $15 million in grants to more than 125 MIT research projects since 2002. Thirty-two projects have spun out of the center as independent start-ups, having collectively raised more than $500 million in outside financing from investors.[30]

A second approach is the lean start-up model made popular by Silicon Valley entrepreneur Steve Blank.[31] This model rejects long, detailed business plans, instead embracing a business model canvas and an iterative process in which minimally viable products are tested and refined until a clear value proposition is demonstrated.[32]

The lean start-up approach has been at the heart of a federal initiative called I-Corps. In a little over five years I-Corps has taught more than seven hundred teams funded by the National Institutes of Health and more than eight hundred teams funded by the National Science Foundation.[33] The teams, which come from 192 universities in forty-four states, are responsible for the creation of more than 320 companies, which have collectively raised more than $83 million in follow-on funding.[34] The National Science Foundation has also established a set of regional nodes to further commercialization efforts through lean start-ups, and the approach has now been widely adopted by entrepreneurship centers around the country.

Almost ten years ago, the two of us founded another approach: a weeklong Faculty Boot Camp on the UNC campus that exposes faculty to entrepreneurial thinking and techniques for increasing the impact of their research. Participants are not limited to scientists but come from across the disciplines, with sociologists and philosophers working alongside chemists and physicians. The week culminates in a "bake-off" in which teams present real-world projects to judges who are often administrators in a position to fund them. The program has expanded to include faculty from outside Chapel Hill, and to date, well over two hundred faculty members have participated.

Last, committed alumni and university endowments are increasingly providing start-up financing for promising campus-based ventures. One model operates like an angel network, in which interested alumni are shown investment opportunities and can choose to invest on a case-by-case basis. Such an approach has been adopted on scores of campuses.[35]

Another approach adopts a grant model, much like the Deshpande Center, in which the university provides start-up funding for promising enterprises without taking equity in exchange.[36] In a hybrid approach, grants and angel investments are combined, as in the Duke Angel Network and the Duke Innovation Fund.[37]

An innovative approach to funding start-ups called Carolina Research Ventures (CRV) has been instituted on the UNC campus. Funded by a $10 million commitment from the school's endowment, the effort focuses on technology ventures across campus. The program is managed by Hatteras Ventures, a nationally known venture capital firm, and a Hatteras partner has an office on campus with a focus on making investments of up to $250,000 in early stage start-ups.

In the first year, the fund made three investments, and the pipeline is much larger than expected, says Mike Dial, a principal at Hatteras. Although Hatteras has invested in UNC-based companies in the past, according to Dial, the CRV setup, in which the university itself holds equity rather than an outside venture capitalist and the fund manager Hatteras has a continuing presence on campus, may contribute to there being a larger than expected pipeline of deals. Carolina Research Ventures also works closely with other campus initiatives designed to support start-ups to create a supportive infrastructure for the commercialization of technology.[38]

Establish Realistic Expectations

The expectation that higher education will be a catalyst for economic development inevitably creates pressure on academic leaders to oversell academia's economic impact and potential to revitalize depressed economic regions. When lobbying for government support, savvy college presidents wrap funding requests in impressive statistics on job creation and increased tax revenue, but some members of the academic community are skeptical of such statistics, and their concerns will find their way into the conversation about rebuilding the partnership.

"I see Mark Zuckerberg has a lot of money, but I don't see [a reversal of] the deindustrialization of the Rust Belt," says Chris Newfield. "I don't see Detroit coming back. I don't see my small town [near Santa Barbara] doing better because there's a university down the road, so I think we really have to rethink this model in a fundamental way." Newfield's primary objection is not to the activities of technology transfer or economic development themselves but rather to how they are funded and whether these activities are draining resources from other areas of the university, principally the humanities.

If technology transfer and economic development are viewed solely as a profit-making activity for the university, Newfield's concerns are well taken. Most research universities earn in royalty- and equity-based revenue only 1–2 percent of what they receive in federal research spending.[39] Typically, this does not produce enough revenue to cover the costs of the tech transfer office, and so those costs are subsidized from elsewhere in the organization. Most of the public benefit of tech transfer accrues in the form of new jobs and tax revenue that do not directly benefit the university. Acknowledging this fact and clearly making the case for technology transfer as a tool to improve science and retain faculty as well as contribute to the public good—while frankly acknowledging that tech transfer takes resources from other activities—is a better approach than overselling its economic benefits.[40]

Newfield's second problem is that the public invests in the early stages of technology development through research funding and indirect subsidies of the commercialization effort, but then very little of the direct economic benefit flows back to the university. "We want to do partnerships," he says, "that are fair to all the parties, including the public that lost money on this for the first twenty years. We should be plowing this back through the tax system or through direct . . . clawbacks."

Again, Newfield is correct that the inventors, entrepreneurs, and investors get most of the benefit if the technology starts to produce revenue. There is a reason for that: the development of these technologies is highly risky, and few result in any profit, much less the billion-dollar unicorns that the press likes to focus on. Only the lure of substantial profit will entice investors to support early stage scientific endeavors. Yet huge returns on university scientific research are few and far between, and the success of those ventures is not predictable. Technology transfer and economic development activities must be undertaken because they are expected by the public and, in some instances, required by law, but expecting a significant economic return on these activities is unrealistic.

Newfield's objections raise an important conundrum for university leaders. On the one hand, the public and politicians expect university research to catalyze economic activity and improve the quality of life. On the other, a significant voice inside the university believes that funding such activities undercuts more important priorities. Although we believe that the forces pushing universities to produce more economic impact will only intensify, the conversation must involve transparency about the real costs and the likely returns both to the university and to the public at large.

One significant risk that needs to be managed is the pressure that the evolving system places on the quality of research. The pressure to get grants and publish high-profile papers already sets up circumstances where highly novel research is overvalued, thereby creating incentives for scientists to publish studies with insufficient statistical validity (often referred to as "underpowered") that may not withstand further experimentation.[41] The addition of financial pressure and the associated media and administrative attention that comes with it has the potential to exacerbate this problem.

UNIVERSITIES AS ENGINES

We used the word "engine" in the title of our first book for a reason. We wanted to highlight the ability of the university to drive innovation, but universities operate as economic engines in ways that go beyond new technologies to include job creation and other aspects of economic activity. We saw in the previous chapter the enormous economic activity associated with academic medicine in the realms of patient care and research. It would be hard to find a university that has not at some point called itself an engine of something—usually something related to economic growth or prosperity. This lexicon is nothing new—Vannevar Bush used it in 1945—but it goes back even further, to the Morrill Act's call for the "practical education of the industrial classes."

Over all of this time, however, university leaders have told two different stories. To the politicians and trustees, the story is about the university as an engine of economic growth and entrepreneurship. To much of the faculty, the story is one of free inquiry and the pursuit of knowledge. As we set the stage for the conversation that rebuilds the partnership, these two stories need to be reconciled so that support of one narrative does not come at the expense of the other.

{ 9

The Case for Both Basic Research and Entrepreneurship

In our first book we argued that "the bill had come due" and that universities would increasingly be expected to embrace entrepreneurial thinking in their teaching and research. In the years since that book was published, the intensity of these expectations has only increased. As we said in the introduction to this volume, we are, if anything, worried that the pendulum has swung too far in the direction of innovation and entrepreneurship, as almost every university has such an initiative. Striking a balance between the worthy objectives of discovering new knowledge and starting new enterprises that create jobs and economic development has become a critical part of rebuilding the partnership.

The concern that the stampede to innovation and entrepreneurship has gone too far is legitimate, because universities are still, in essence, called to produce and distribute knowledge that may or may not have immediate application. The right approach is for universities to embrace innovation and entrepreneurship, but not at the expense of other important university priorities. By having clear policies and great services for technology transfer and translation, the university can avoid being a stumbling block for realizing the potential of scientific discovery and economic growth while assuring all concerned that commercialization will not have a corrupting influence on the academic enterprise. Now more than ever, we believe that the time is right for colleges and universities to undertake the internal changes necessary to create a culture supportive of innovation and entrepreneurship.

Jonathan Cole put this well: "I think there is a tension that still exists between what I would call an emphasis on fundamental knowledge and that which is a kind of practical use and utility. I don't see those as incompatible. We have a track record over seventy years of producing some enormously important discoveries, including basic ones."

WHY BASIC RESEARCH?

We begin with basic research because it is core to the mission of higher education and it builds a foundation for innovation and entrepreneurship. Four key rationales anchor the bargain by which faculty are given the autonomy to conduct curiosity-driven basic research. Although many readers may view all four of them as important, faculty likely view the first as most important while trustees and policymakers are typically most concerned with the last. Regardless of their relative importance, together they form the fundamental rationale for basic research.

Knowledge for Knowledge's Sake Is a Good unto Itself

This rationale is embraced not only by philosophers and theoretical physicists but by academics generally. It is why many were attracted to academia in the first place. Contemplating, researching, testing, and writing about ideas requires habits of mind that academics hold in high regard. They are the same habits of mind that produced the great works of art and scholarship and that animated the creation of democracy and religion, and the university is one of the last places in our society where this sort of thinking and research is encouraged and valued.

New Knowledge Is a Good unto Itself

The creation of new knowledge is a service to society, and training others in the practice of curating and generating new knowledge is a core part of the academic mission. Knowledge of life and matter is the basis of science, and understanding culture and behavior builds empathy and reduces conflict. For at least the past two centuries, most new knowledge has been generated in universities, so this rationale suggests that academic research must be sustained to provide a usable understanding of a changing world.

Innovators of the Future Need Our Knowledge

We cannot know what knowledge will be useful in the future, so it is the responsibility of academicians to follow their curiosity and document their findings. Their work will be the basis for cures and technologies beyond the imaginations of those who did the original research that opened the door to these innovations. A tangible example is a project at IBM to create a supercomputer that can read all of the scientific papers on cancer and recommend therapeutic interventions to physicians.[1]

The Work We Do Is Useful Now

Academic researchers can often commercialize their findings simultaneously with the execution of their curiosity-driven research. Researchers such as Bob Langer, a professor at MIT, and Joe DeSimone, at UNC—both of whom we profiled in our previous book—built large research efforts inside and outside of the university and created economic activity and intense public interest in their work.

We believe the tension along this continuum—from the pursuit of knowledge for knowledge's sake to readily applicable discovery—is inevitable and ultimately positive, so long as it is understood. The outside world is unlikely to accept a focus on basic knowledge as a primary rationale for providing tax dollars and tax exemptions to universities. Academics are unlikely to submit to purely pecuniary and instrumentalist motives for inquiry. So discussions of the relative value of basic research versus applied knowledge will continue, as they should. We believe that succeeding at innovation and entrepreneurship is academia's best strategy for keeping both in balance.

Our interviews highlighted these disparate points of view. "I think the rapid expectation [of immediate results] is quite bad," says Chris Newfield. "I have direct experience with industry folks that worked with scientists that basically misled their investors about the time frame. The investors panicked and cut them off and their companies died, and I trace that back to not having set realistic expectations at the beginning about whether we're doing basic or applied research."

All of the trustees we talked to took the other side. "I think that universities are still today thought of as places to create professionals and knowledge workers, and not enough are being trained as forward thinkers and entrepreneurs and innovators," says Washington University's Gene Kahn. Lowry Caudill, a trustee at UNC–Chapel Hill, made an important point about the nature of research today. "Most of the basic research in the United States is being done inside universities today and not in industry as it used to be fifty years ago," he says, "so if we don't unleash the potential inside our universities and apply that new knowledge and these innovations, then we're in trouble nationally. There is a national strategic issue here, and we have to change the way we do things in the university because the days of going to conferences and writing papers will still go on, but it's much more than that now. It's having an impact in the world on what's happening here and how to use this scholarship, how to use these innovations and do something with it."

WHY INNOVATION AND ENTREPRENEURSHIP?

As reinforced by the statements of the trustees we talked to, the renewed partnership with the public must include an expectation that universities that conduct basic research also engage in applied research aimed at solving real-world problems and teach students how to do the same. Entrepreneurship centers and accelerators designed to commercialize academic research are already required activities at virtually all colleges and universities. Government agencies such as the National Science Foundation and the National Institutes of Health often require grant requests to contain a plan for commercialization, including a non-academic partner to manage the commercial side of the research.

The factors that currently drive innovation and entrepreneurship in higher education include the following.

Applied Research Is More Easily Explained

Telling the story of university research is a struggle. Mainstream media write cursory stories about basic research, but only when the research has immediate impact. Universities produce magazines and websites filled with press releases about research, but they are rarely read. Trustees and alumni always ask, "Why don't I ever hear about the great things going on at the university?" What they mean is, why don't I hear about exciting research on National Public Radio or read about it in the *National Review*? Commercialization of research (or demonstrating real-world applications for some advance in knowledge) solves this problem by putting a human face on what might otherwise be a difficult story to tell. Explaining the effect of trauma on the human brain is useful but not nearly as engaging as explaining how to protect young children from concussions while playing football or lacrosse.

Teaching Entrepreneurial Thinking Is Now Required

Most undergraduates do not enter college expecting to become entrepreneurs. While Stanford and MIT and a host of other schools have established themselves as proving grounds for budding entrepreneurs, market research shows that most entering undergraduates expect to attend professional school or obtain a job in a large company on graduation. Only after they enroll do some students realize they would like to work in, or start, a new enterprise. As a result of student demand and the expectations of their parents and the public at large, innovation and entrepreneurship have evolved from a desirable component of the college curriculum to a course of study that is increasingly fundamental to the institution.

The integration of the study and development of the entrepreneurial mindset into the curriculum became more accepted once this approach was distinguished from pure commercialization. Just as the scientific method can be applied to almost any real-world problem, disciplined approaches to innovation and entrepreneurship have application in the sciences, the arts, the humanities, and any other activity that requires a sustainable operating model to survive. And as jobs at large companies change in response to a dynamic business environment, a flexible, entrepreneurial mindset will increasingly be a requirement for success.

Lowry Caudill considers this a mandate to "work with the students to get them thinking in an entrepreneurial way. How do you recognize an opportunity, how do you develop your strategy, how do you develop your resources to make it happen, and how do you then measure it?" Caudill believes that entrepreneurial thinking gives students a way to understand how basic knowledge operates in the wider world.

Defining entrepreneurship as a way of thinking, and not merely as an approach to commercializing an idea or enterprise, has a profound impact on the way entrepreneurship is taught. Simply put, the teaching of entrepreneurial thinking as a useful habit of mind for twenty-first-century students should not be confined to the business school. Rather, it should infuse teaching across the curriculum. Such an approach should not come at the expense of robust offerings in the arts and sciences but rather should be complementary to a liberal education. The two of us have consistently advocated that entrepreneurship should be a minor (but not a major) in the arts and sciences so that majors throughout the college can be exposed to entrepreneurial thinking.

Entrepreneurship programs certainly have a place in business schools, but the relationship between the student and the business school is generally more transactional in nature. It is a school whose mission is more vocationally focused. Nevertheless, business school administrators and alumni often want the business school to "own" the university's entrepreneurship imprimatur, which causes tension with campuswide efforts to infuse entrepreneurial thinking into the culture of the entire institution. This tension can be channeled productively by adopting a university-wide approach that recognizes the place of entrepreneurship not only as an important skill for a variety of activities and enterprises but also as a habit of mind that is useful in virtually any walk of life.

Faculty Need Help to Commercialize Their Research

As successful companies are increasingly spun out of universities, ambitious faculty members want to try their hand at commercializing their research. The notoriety and financial rewards that result are seductive, and once a university entrepreneur hits it big, other faculty are moved to seek the same outcome. More and more, a successful academic career in the sciences involves multiple federal grants, a large research group, papers in the glossy journals (*Cell*, *Science*, and *Nature*), and a start-up company. As star faculty seek to add start-ups to their portfolios, universities must provide support if they hope to retain them.

In addition to faculty retention, support of technology transfer is often justified for the profits it can produce for the institution. In reality, those profits can be elusive. A few universities—Northwestern is one example— have generated substantial revenue from university-based research, and every university president hopes for such an outcome.[2] It is a mistake to expect lightning to strike in this way, however. Only once or twice a decade does a university hit it big in the realm of tech transfer, and the odds against its happening are steep. This is not to say that universities should ignore the revenue. Even modest profits can supplement faculty incomes, money for departments, and funds to operate the technology transfer office. But universities should be clear-eyed about what is a realistic return: at best a predictable revenue stream from royalties, the occasional return on start-up equity, and—only if they are very lucky—a larger payoff.

WHY COMMERCIALIZATION IS SO DIFFICULT IN A UNIVERSITY SETTING

Commercialization is tough no matter the setting, but for a number of reasons, it is particularly difficult in academia. First, academic ideas often are not sufficiently developed. Most university researchers are focused on examining and understanding something, and not on producing an Edison-style invention that pays off quickly. Even if a researcher is doing applied research, university-generated ideas are typically "too early." That is, the concept has been tested in the lab by graduate students with makeshift equipment and a few replications. This doesn't translate to an immediate application.

For instance, in the drug business, university researchers might show that something worked in cells or maybe in a mouse, but that is no guarantee that it will work in a large animal or a human. These latter steps are very costly and time consuming. Typically, they take place outside of the university and are conducted by professionals who are highly compensated.

An additional barrier to establishing productive partnerships between higher education and businesses has to do with the narratives that drive the two worlds. Research scientists would say that understanding something is the ultimate goal. The world of packaging and presenting a discovery made in a lab is foreign to them. The business world believes that success favors individuals who can frame the discovery for the marketplace, present it skillfully so that it appeals to potential investors, negotiate hard, and make gutsy decisions. It is not enough to find a molecule that can be a billion-dollar drug: it is not a billion-dollar drug until it has been *sold* for a billion dollars. Most scientists have no idea how to sell a billion-dollar drug.

MAKING INNOVATION AND
ENTREPRENEURSHIP A REALITY

Innovation and entrepreneurship have become the flavor of the week on campuses throughout the United States and abroad. It is hard to find a college website that does not contain the words. The European Union has established numerous commissions and initiatives to encourage entrepreneurship in higher education.[3] Interest is also strong in China, where many of the top universities are focused on integrating an entrepreneurial mindset into their curricula.[4] Too often, however, campus initiatives focus on creating a structure rather than changing the culture. Structural change is, more often than not, temporary while cultural change is enduring and grows and evolves as part of the lifeblood of an institution. Ultimately, a rebuilt partnership will demand such cultural change, and to that end, we have seen several best practices emerge on our own campuses and elsewhere.

Define Entrepreneurship Broadly

According to the late Peter Drucker, entrepreneurship is not a science or an art but a defined practice that can be applied to a variety of problems and opportunities.[5] An entrepreneurial approach can be just as important in a social, artistic, or scientific endeavor as it is in a commercial enterprise. Moreover, as we discussed earlier, a liberal education is ideal training for the innovative thinking that entrepreneurship, broadly defined, requires.

Embracing this point is critical to success in an academic environment. Anthropologists and historians, who may not be enthusiastic about something they see as a business practice, can be engaged by social or artistic entrepreneurs whose values are more aligned with theirs. Social entrepreneurs have great appeal as speakers on university campuses, and their presence helps define entrepreneurial thinking broadly. Faculty seminars and workshops on the entrepreneurial mindset aimed at the arts and humanities are another way to define entrepreneurship as a set of tools and not a set of values. Ideally, entrepreneurial thinking becomes integrated broadly in the curriculum as part of a liberal arts education so English majors and musicians also graduate with the necessary tools to turn their big ideas into reality.

As we mentioned earlier, a key impediment to such an approach is the tendency in academia to locate all teaching of entrepreneurship in one school or department, typically business or engineering. Many grant funders, most specifically the Kauffman Foundation, have been strident in their opposition to this siloed approach because such a structure decreases the chances that the larger campus will be exposed to these important ideas and techniques.

We believe that the best practice is to encourage coordination and interaction among schools and departments as well as to undertake a diverse set of programs and approaches that are generated from the bottom up with no attempt to create a single administrative structure in which they all fit. In a perfect world, traditional faculty, entrepreneurs-in-residence, and others interested in innovation will develop multidisciplinary teams and other similar structures to teach techniques and approaches that give all interested students and faculty the skills required to turn ideas into reality.

Open the Tent

Welcoming people who have worked at least part of their careers in the private sector to the academic enterprise has a profound effect on any institution. First, they can act as mediators between academics and businesspeople, who are driven by different narratives. They can reassure scientists who get antsy in the latter stages of negotiations when the business folks start pounding the table over the last few terms. They can also reassure businesspeople that scientists understand the need for an actual product that can be sold and a path for selling it.

At Washington University, we brought individuals with experience in both academia and business into administrative positions running the technology transfer operation, the drug discovery center, and the entrepreneurship education center. The University of North Carolina created the position of entrepreneur-in-residence, making room for individuals with deep experience outside of academia to work closely with people on the inside, often in teams.[6] We found that in addition to being generally competent at their jobs, people from the outside dramatically affect the culture. They are accustomed to relatively short time horizons, and as a result they speed up decision making. They often have an extensive network of contacts that can be extraordinarily valuable to academics and students alike. Conveniently, they are typically not interested in a tenured position and therefore do not compete against academics who have taken the more traditional path. Often they are at a point in their careers where they do not require a large salary, although it is important that they be on the payroll.

The key is to find entrepreneurs and others with nonacademic experience who respect the academic enterprise, are effective in working with students and faculty, and have a passion for innovation and entrepreneurship. The results can be unpredictable, and at times exasperating, but the ultimate outcome can be that entrepreneurs will change the culture in ways that creating centers or reorganizing departments cannot.

Infuse Innovation and Entrepreneurship throughout the Curriculum

Teaching the entrepreneurial mindset and the skills required for innovation in one department or school is a critical error that grows out of the belief that entrepreneurship is merely another way of describing a commercial enterprise. And such a structure inoculates the rest of the campus from coming to grips with the need to integrate entrepreneurial thinking throughout the curriculum. When innovation and entrepreneurship are defined broadly as a way of thinking that can be applied to virtually any problem, significant changes throughout the curriculum can take place without threatening the ideals of a traditional liberal education. Such changes involve multidisciplinary, problem-centered courses and seminars; an emphasis on maker spaces, where students are encouraged to work not only with ideas but also with physical materials; and experiential learning, where internships and other off-campus experiences are integrated into the curriculum.

DETERMINING SUCCESS

As the conversation about rebuilding the partnership continues, university administrators will inevitably highlight what they claim to be successful initiatives aimed at innovation and entrepreneurship. Real success, though, will involve a cultural change that will better equip the institution to teach and tackle the major problems of the twenty-first century. Determining whether the culture of the institution is actually changing can be difficult. In our own experience, the following are signs of real cultural change:

- Classes in innovation and entrepreneurship are oversubscribed, and the only impediments to growth are the availability of instructors and classroom space.
- Entrepreneurs-in-residence have been appointed in such places as the medical school, pharmacy school, school of social work, and even school of public health.
- Students have created social entrepreneurship incubators, housed in the student center.
- The revised curriculum in arts and sciences incorporates innovation, entrepreneurship, and problem-based learning.
- Faculty from the arts and humanities are teaching or guest lecturing in the entrepreneurship program, and artistic, social, and scientific entrepreneurs are part of the curriculum in traditional departments.
- Deans and other campus leaders have entrepreneurial experience.
- Innovation and entrepreneurial thinking are central pillars of a capital campaign.

In most conversations about rebuilding the partnership with the public, the need for innovation and entrepreneurial thinking will not be a serious question: that train has left the station. Nevertheless, achieving the real cultural change entailed in becoming an entrepreneurial university is tough and will not be completed until entrepreneurial thinking is integrated with the other values that make American higher education unique. This does not have to be a zero-sum game. We are convinced the requirements of a twenty-first-century education that addresses the legitimate concerns of a college's various constituencies can be achieved without sacrificing the fundamental values at the heart of American higher education.

{ 10

An Education
and a Job

Although nothing is more central to rebuilding the partnership than confronting the expectation that a college degree will lead to a good job and a secure financial future, academia and the public have fundamental disagreements about how this responsibility should be fulfilled. Most students, parents, lawmakers, and trustees would place getting a good job at or near the top of any list of important outcomes for higher education. Many in the academy believe that focusing chiefly on employment cheapens the goals of liberal education in producing the habits of mind for engaged citizenship and personal fulfillment.[1]

Still, the expectation of employment after graduation is reasonable and is so fundamental to the rationale for American higher education that it would be impossible to walk it back. When we framed the issue for Chris Newfield, he responded, "We are on the hook." Academia must accept this employment imperative and succeed both in helping graduates find a job and—at the same time—in intellectualizing the experience, so that the lofty purposes of education are not undermined. As Jeff Selingo told us, "I don't think higher education is just about getting the job and making money, but I definitely think now that we are starting to talk much more specifically about the value proposition of higher education. People are starting to focus on: What am I paying for? What are the outputs?"

Empirical studies show that getting a good job—or a better job and making more money—is why most students go to college.[2] A recent conversation with twenty first-year students confirmed that a job on graduation and a secure financial future with a "nice house and not living paycheck to paycheck" were their prime motivators for getting a college degree. As one student said, "If I give up four years of my life and pay four years of tuition, I expect to find a job when I graduate." As the conversation progressed, other motivations came out, such as a desire to make a difference in the world or to lead a "good life," but these more aspirational goals were voiced most often by outstanding students who will have their pick of career opportunities.

This concern with economic security is also reflected in the popularity of career-oriented courses in business, journalism, public health, and other areas that integrate real-world insights, skills, and experience with academic rigor. Conversely, courses in the liberal arts that do not have a ready-made connection to the world of work have suffered in enrollment and funding.[3] "The traditional deal," says Newfield, "is [that] we make your child ready for a middle-class job and along the way may give them capacities of self-understanding, civic and cultural participation, and creativity and pleasure—kind of in descending order. That is still what the voting public wants to get from the system and there's much more focus on getting younger people into the employment world." Carol Folt sees it similarly: "Every time our faculty stand up and say, 'It's not about getting jobs,' I cringe," she says, "because I think, 'Why shouldn't the family care if their kids get jobs?'"

"This is not just about a career and an income," says United Negro College Fund CEO Michael Lomax, "but you cannot dismiss meaningful employment and compensation. You have to recognize that for a formerly enslaved people, work has been central to our experience in this country, and our work and effort have been devalued and dehumanized. So much of what we are pursuing in our aspirations for education is to be able to have meaningful work which is valued and rewarded because we as full human beings are valued and rewarded. That economic element of the education has extraordinary value, but so does the role that it plays in preparing us to be full citizens, something we have also fought for so that we can engage in the democracy as full citizens and take our rightful places within that democratic process so that we can also fully develop and appreciate our intellectual and spiritual capabilities." We asked Lomax to respond to the criticism that emphasizing career outcomes reduces higher education to job training. "I think that is trivializing the issue," he said, "and where's the empathy?"

THE DISCONNECTS BETWEEN ACADEMIA
AND THE PRIVATE SECTOR

On the critical question of whether a college education prepares students for the work world, academia and the private sector could hardly be further apart. Whereas 96 percent of chief academic officers think that the graduates of their institution are properly equipped for employment out of college, only 11 percent of business leaders agree.[4] This stunning disconnect is the backdrop of the discussion that follows.

Unemployment among college graduates is surprisingly low. Among recent graduates in civil engineering and nursing, the rates are 2.8 percent and 2 percent, respectively, and among liberal arts majors, the rate is 5.8 percent.[5] Considering highly ranked colleges, only 5 to 7 percent of recent graduates are unemployed six months after graduation.[6] (Graduates who attended for-profit institutions have higher unemployment rates.[7]) The percentage of recent graduates who are working at a position that does not require a college degree is estimated to be as high as 44 percent, but this underemployment number falls to one-third over time as graduates gain experience in the workplace. By other measures of underemployment, the number is as low as 19.8 percent, and the underemployed graduates typically occupy better-paying administrative jobs.[8]

Qualitative factors also influence these data. Many graduates take low-paying jobs in order to get a foot in the door or to explore various options in an effort to find particularly meaningful work. Others are burned out and take a year off before looking for a job in earnest. Students who are willing to live with a degree of uncertainty and ambiguity often eventually obtain more interesting opportunities than those who attempt to have employment tied down well before graduation.

Not all students are in a financial situation that allows them to do this, however. For many, getting a well-paying job on graduation is an economic necessity. Given shifting student demographics and higher levels of student debt, the percentage of students for whom a good first job is critical will likely increase over time. This suggests another reason for getting the employment imperative right: as universities pursue economic diversity in their student populations, the importance of helping graduates obtain a good first job only increases because these new entrants will not be able to rely on family connections for their first jobs.

Getting that first job is important but not the biggest challenge. Graduates today face the ongoing and often daunting task of navigating a career that could involve upwards of twenty job changes.[9] The obsession with the first job obscures the issue, which is the radical and constant change taking place in the workplace. Just think about the job of a print journalist. Today, traditional writing skills must be combined with social media savvy and the ability to navigate a newsroom that operates around the clock. The same need to adjust to profound change applies to professions as disparate as surgeons, who now employ robots as essential tools, and auto mechanics, who are more likely to replace circuits than parts. What is demanded of higher education is both preparation and support for obtaining a good job on graduation and an education that equips a graduate to thrive in a rapidly changing work environment.

This accelerated change in the workforce and the nature of work itself reinforces the adage that a college degree prepares students for jobs that do not exist yet. In our own experience, the most exciting opportunities for recent graduates did not exist when they entered college. One of our students, a public policy major, now works for Google on news story authentication. Another, a chemistry major, is now working on a more efficient form of 3-D printing at a start-up. It is unlikely that any curriculum can anticipate all of the requirements of those rapidly changing career areas. Even for graduates whose first job is more conventional, the prospect of multiple job changes during their careers suggests a continuous process of retooling.

The ideal of being a lifelong learner is no longer a platitude. It has become an economic necessity, and the academic community is only beginning to understand that traditional teaching methods and curricula must be adapted to develop a twenty-first-century workforce and citizens of an increasingly complex world.

Employers already understand the need for change and the new skills that must be taught, even if academia is still catching up. When asked to rate the attributes they seek on a candidate's résumé, prospective employers rate soft skills such as leadership, ability to work on a team, a strong work ethic, communication skills, and problem solving ability much higher than analytical and quantitative skills, technical competence, and computer skills.[10] And although academic major has the most significant influence on an employer's decision to hire one candidate over another, leadership roles the candidate took in college, participation in extracurricular activities, and a high GPA are also key factors.[11]

As the data show, academics generally believe that they are teaching the very skills that employers seek, yet employers overwhelmingly disagree. Where is the disconnect? We believe that one answer centers on the inability of the traditional lecture to teach adequately all the skills that graduates must have to succeed. Twenty-first-century problems are complex and require diverse teams with different skill sets and points of view to tackle them.

A modern college curriculum should combine traditional course work in a particular discipline with multidisciplinary, problem-based courses that more closely approximate real-world problems. Such an approach has the advantage not only of teaching the soft skills that employers increasingly value but also of leveraging the demonstrable advantages of just-in-time learning in which knowledge is acquired to solve an immediate and pressing problem.[12] A semester-long project—such as how to test water quality at low cost or developing a design for an underused courtyard at a school—can be the foundation of such an approach.[13] Professors go from being authorities conveying knowledge to coaches empowering and encouraging teams to discover and apply knowledge in order to solve a series of problems that reveal themselves over a semester.

In addition to its other advantages, the problem-based approach lends itself to involving experts from inside and outside of academia, to provide both expertise on the particular subject matter and coaching on team dynamics and problem solving. Although such an approach is labor-intensive, our experience—both with a four-hundred-student course on entrepreneurship involving eighty projects and twenty coaches and smaller seminars anchored by semester-long team projects—has convinced us that problem-based learning is a critical component of a twenty-first-century college education. We are consistently told by students that their experience with these sorts of projects is helpful in interviews for their first job, but more important, we are convinced that it prepares them for the many different jobs—some of which do not yet exist—they will encounter during their careers.

A MULTIDIMENSIONAL APPROACH
TO CAREER READINESS

The elements for addressing career readiness are already present in undergraduate education. The Gallup-Purdue index surveyed thirty thousand college graduates and found that nearly four in ten were "highly engaged" at work.[14] The extent of workplace engagement was then correlated with the extent of support and experiential learning in college. In the support area, participants were asked whether (a) at least one professor made them excited about learning, (b) the professors at their school cared about them as a person, or (c) they had a mentor who encouraged their hopes and dreams. In the experiential learning area, participants were asked whether they (a) had an internship that allowed them to apply what they learned in the classroom, (b) worked on a project that took a semester or more to complete, or (c) were extremely active in extracurricular activities and organizations while attending college. The odds of being highly engaged at work were approximately doubled by strong agreement with any of these six measures, but only 3 percent of those surveyed strongly agreed that they had received all six.

The Gallup-Purdue data reveal other interesting findings. The first is that the odds of workplace engagement were the same for graduates of any public or private nonprofit college (the odds were significantly lower for graduates of for-profits). The second is that the effect of the mentor was the same regardless of whether the mentor was a full professor or another staff member. And the effect of choice of major was modest; in fact, arts and social science majors were more likely to feel engaged in the workplace than science or business majors.

These findings provide a strong foundation to build on. If students and their parents are expected to pay an increasing portion of the cost of an education—and often go into debt to do so—they expect that a graduate will be well positioned to get a good job and well prepared for the changing nature of the workplace. An unprecedented amount of time and energy is currently being devoted to this challenge and some best practices are emerging. We describe several here.

Be Transparent about the Credential

Notwithstanding the overwhelming evidence that a college degree is worth it, not all degrees provide equal short-term benefits, and as increasing amounts of information become available, colleges should expect that students will want to make an informed decision.[15] If a degree program is designed with a particular occupation in mind—for example, law enforcement or cybersecurity—applicants should be asking about the percentage of graduates who get jobs in the field, the average starting salary, and the average salary five years after graduation. It makes little sense to enroll in a highly targeted course of study if the expected salary is not commensurate with the cost of the degree. For more academic courses of study, students are asking harder questions than ever before. Specifically, they want to know if helping them get a good job is high on the list of a school's institutional priorities.

Schools will need to be increasingly clear about the answer. Some schools may choose to minimize explicit career education and focus on learning for its own sake; as we have said here repeatedly, there is a strong argument that a traditional liberal arts education is great preparation for almost any career, and that has been validated in many surveys. Such an approach assumes, though, that armed with their degree and the assistance of a career-counseling center, graduates should have no trouble finding a job. If this is the case, supporting data should provide the percentage of graduates with jobs six months after graduation and job satisfaction figures five years out.[16] Schools who integrate career training and planning deeply into their curriculum should make that clear as well, and should validate their approach with hard data.

What is most important is that the terms of the heretofore implicit arrangement between a school and its students be articulated and understood. If job readiness is not the primary goal of a school's curriculum, that should be set out from the outset and the validity of the approach should be demonstrated. On the other hand, if landing a good job is the primary driver of a degree program, students are entitled to know to what extent the goal is typically achieved.

Involve Nontraditional Instructors

We have long been proponents of involving people with experience in the private sector in the key functions of the university as a way of improving the curriculum and increasing the impact of research.[17] Their presence on campus can also help students prepare for a good job and understand the challenges of the changing workplace. Professors with experience outside academia bring with them a perspective on developing the hard and soft skills that complement a traditional degree, and they often have experience teaching such skills. Nonacademics impart a sense of urgency in decision-making that is more typical of the world outside of academia, and that is a valuable habit of mind for students to learn.

Most important, professors with real-world experience have a host of contacts and relationships that can help students find internships and good first jobs. This is particularly important as the percentage of first-generation college students increases. The maxim "It's a small world" does not necessarily apply to them, and higher education will be required to perform the door-opening function that is traditionally done by friends and family of wealthier and better-connected students. As part of opening the door they also need help with interviewing and networking techniques that often help land that good first job.[18]

While it may be unsettling to career academics, the Gallup-Purdue finding that the efficacy of a mentor in college is not related to their academic status is significant: the mentor need not be an academic star. This is a liberating idea once accepted; nontraditional academic appointments can be an extremely useful tool in developing mentoring capacity.

Develop Innovative Faculty Enrichment

It is not easy to transition from the traditional lecture method to a more problem-based form of teaching that develops skills employers want. It requires leadership from the top, focused training workshops, and financial support for implementation. As we have discussed, faculty rule their domain inside the classroom for good reasons. Demanding that they change their way of teaching will meet resistance. Convincing faculty that such a change is in the interest of their students has a higher likelihood of success, especially in appealing to the desire to serve students of lower wealth.

This can happen most often through the leadership of deans and department chairs and through the development of faculty workshops that embrace these new ideas. Weeklong faculty workshops that focus on problem-based teaching, design thinking, and innovation and entrepreneurship are an effective way to inspire the faculty to move in this direction. For example, since 1984 Babson College has been teaching teams of academics and entrepreneurs how to teach entrepreneurship.

One key to the success of such workshops is an invitation from the president or a dean to participate and the offer of financial and other support to implement the lessons learned from the experience. Course development grants, adjustments to teaching loads, and other similar incentives increase the likelihood of follow-through. A detailed, module-based course curriculum will allow a professor from any discipline to adopt a problem-based approach or insert other elements from the workshop directly into an existing course. Writing a new curriculum with aspirational goals about career readiness is a start, but actually implementing those good intentions is the challenge, and that will not happen without an intentional plan for faculty training.

"The challenge is back on the academy to be less defensive, less protective of the status quo," says Lomax, "and to think about what can we teach that helps people navigate diverse social and cultural environments. What can we teach that enables people to persist in problem-solving that seems almost impossible to achieve? How do we enable people to communicate effectively with others in the work environment of the twenty-first century? I certainly do not think that the goal is to produce a bunch of robots; that is not what we are doing. I think this is an inflection point for education, not just in the U.S., but around the world, because we have different kinds of tools. We are either going to have humanists and others in the academy a part of that, or it is going to happen without them. That is what would be scary for me: that the people who are the guardians of our values and the best of what we have created would isolate themselves from the marketplace."

Integrate Internships and Experiential Learning

An off-campus internship or some other form of experiential learning is as important to today's students as an introductory science or English course, another point emphasized in the Gallup-Purdue data. Increasingly, internships have become a degree requirement, and this trend is accelerating as pressure mounts on institutions to prepare students better for the workforce.

Internship programs are people-intensive and difficult to scale, but schools like Northeastern University in Boston prove that it can be done. Northeastern, a pioneer in experiential education, integrates what they called co-ops into their curriculum. They alternate two six-month co-op experiences for credit with six months of on-campus learning over a four-year period—or three co-op experiences over a five-year period. For a recent year, the school made eleven thousand co-op placements in 133 countries. Other colleges and universities, such as the University of Cincinnati (the birthplace of cooperative education) and Knox College, have also embraced experiential learning and thoroughly integrated it into the curriculum.

A commitment to require experiential learning cannot be successful without dedicated resources and an adjustment in the requirements for a degree. At the very least, this means hiring internship advisers who provide support and leads for students. Northeastern University assigns one adviser per every hundred students—a ratio that makes mandatory internships an expensive proposition at large universities.[19]

Small stipends for summer undergraduate research is another relatively cost-effective way to encourage experiential learning, and this approach has the advantage of relying on traditional academics who are well positioned to manage such an effort. Providing stipends in connection with unpaid internships enables students of all backgrounds to participate and lowers the stigma of an unpaid internship.

Many schools involve alumni in helping with internship placement. BrownConnect is a an initiative at Brown University that enables students to seek out career mentorship from alumni through networking opportunities and internships.[20]

Ultimately, if experiential education is to become a requirement, it will have to involve course credit and therefore a recognition by the school that valid learning can take place outside the classroom. With proper attention and consensus-building, though, experiential learning can be embraced by the academy. When we asked Newfield how he viewed experiential learning, he said, "Positively, it just has to be intellectualized." Newfield believes that with the right amount of writing and assessment, the experiences can be conceptually meaningful. Then, he says, "There's metacognition and reflection involved in the experience. I think that's fantastic."

Address the Career Issue Early

At Wake Forest University, Andy Chan, the director of the Office of Personal and Career Development, addresses incoming students and their parents during orientation and assures them that if they follow their interests and passions while in college, he and his thirty or so colleagues will look after their employability.[21] Chan, who also manages initiatives in innovation and entrepreneurship, oversees a concierge-like effort that involves internships, problem-based classes, and alumni involvement—along with résumé-building and interviewing skills—to achieve a track record of at least 95 percent full employment (or graduate school enrollment) within six months following graduation.[22] In Chan's view, if the liberal arts are to be preserved, they have a responsibility to help humanities and social sciences majors translate their studies to the work world.

For Wake Forest, great career services are a strategic imperative, and they have proven to be a valuable tool for student recruitment and parental involvement, even translating into development opportunities, and Wake Forest is by no means alone. At the University of Chicago, 80 percent of first-year students engage with career services, and the president of Wesleyan, Michael Roth, has made coaching first-year students on thoughtful career choices a priority for the school.[23]

What is driving these initiatives? In a word, *parents*, or—when it comes to nontraditional students—the students themselves. University leaders such as Wake Forest president Nathan Hatch are clear when they say that schools must demonstrate a commitment to career services early in a student's time at the university and can no longer prioritize the function "somewhere just below parking."[24] As President Roth of Wesleyan puts it, "[Parents are] used to kids getting what they want, and they expect that to happen at graduation."[25]

Admittedly, addressing career development early thrusts the subject into the spotlight, sometimes with unintended consequences, such as anxious parents contacting faculty demanding to know what a particular major can do for their child once he or she graduates. More fundamentally, thoughtful scholars worry that elevating issues of job readiness so early in the process overly emphasizes the strictly transactional nature of a college education and marginalizes the societal importance of an educated citizenry. The reality is that every major trend in higher education—changing demographics, strained business models, and the challenges and opportunities of new technology—argue for a proactive approach to job readiness, and the sooner in a student's career, the better.

Set Goals and Monitor Results

If there is one thing we have been consistent about throughout this book, and in *Engines of Innovation* as well, it is that schools must be intentional about the results they hope to achieve and must create meaningful measures to track their progress. "It's complicated" is no excuse for failing to develop useful metrics. When it comes to career readiness and the related issue of the value of a degree, national comparative data are readily available, and schools should assume that parents and students will be familiar with it.

For instance, the Education Trust produces College Results Online, an online tool that provides information on graduation rates, postcollege earnings, debt, and loan repayment rates for nearly every four-year college or university in the country.[26] College Scorecard, produced by the U.S. Department of Education, provides similar information in graphic format that facilitates comparisons. These tools set baseline measures for comparing performance among schools on such measures as average annual cost, graduation rate, and salary after attending. The Gallup-Purdue index is updated every year, and individual institutions also collect current data on related topics.

THE JOBS DISCUSSION IS HERE TO STAY

The conversation around college and jobs is often highly charged. Republican politicians are quick to chastise the liberal arts, even though many of them received liberal arts degrees from selective schools.[27] Even Barack Obama—who was himself a nontraditional academic at the University of Chicago before becoming president—chastised the art history major as poor career preparation. What all of this means is that it polls well to say negative things about a liberal arts education.

Nevertheless, objective data show that these politically charged statements misstate the situation. For example, workplace success is *not* strongly related to chosen major. And many of the most traditional elements of a liberal arts education—such as being inspired by a professor or learning flexible interpersonal skills—are highly predictive of future success. Indeed, much of the traditional academic coursework has long involved classes that offer in-depth experiences that go beyond didactic learning. The humanities seminar—the original flipped classroom—has long involved group discussion, deep reading on one's own time, and writing about complex issues and problems. Lab courses in science, performing arts courses, and undergraduate research all have elements of what is now called problem-based learning.

In the last four chapters, we have laid out the four areas where we feel the evolving expectations of the public are irreversible—academic medicine, economic development, innovation and entrepreneurship, and career readiness. We believe that by facing up to these obligations and making them explicit, colleges and universities can accumulate the political capital needed to strengthen the partnership with America and set the stage for a future era of even greater success.

Framing the Conversation

The conversation to rebuild the partnership with the public is well under way all across the United States. It is taking place in Wisconsin, where reductions in tenure protections are indirectly being traded for increased financial support and the board of regents is calling for more candidates from industry to be considered to lead the state's universities.[1] It is taking place in California, where severe budget cuts challenge what is generally accepted as the nation's leading public university system. It is taking place in virtually every state legislature, as traditionally bipartisan support for higher education erodes in the face of negative polling numbers among older and Republican voters.[2] It is taking place at small liberal arts colleges faced with declining enrollments and the economic reality of having to change, merge with another institution, or close. And most notably, it is reflected in the massive tax reform bill of 2017.

The issues being discussed will not be resolved uniformly. The history of American higher education has been an evolutionary process, from its beginnings at Harvard in 1636, to the creation of the first state university in 1789, to the initiation of major governmental funding initiatives in 1862, to the present, when public and private funding are imperiled as a result of lack of trust. Though the results of the conversation will not be uniform, the participants involved and the views advanced are predictable.

Providing a preview of what to expect, we believe, will be helpful to all with an interest in how these critical issues are ultimately resolved. What follows is a description of a fictional, but realistic, gathering convened to begin the process of rebuilding the partnership between a public university and its constituents.

A FICTIONAL CONVERSATION

The Participants

The meeting was convened by Steven Nichols, the chair of the board of trustees of the university, an affluent entrepreneur and a major financial supporter of the university. Other participants include Gregory Grantham, the long-time chancellor of the university; Sylvia Stem, the chair of the faculty and a tenured professor in the department of biology; Mary Madison Darien, the president of the student body; Roy Capps, the newly elected Democratic governor; and Robert Radford, the Republican leader of the state legislature. Nichols invited Judith Berg, a university of Pennsylvania economist—who has written extensively on American higher education—to attend as a consultant to the group.

The Background

Nichols asked Professor Berg to set the stage with some background and context. Berg laid out the informal compact that has traditionally existed between higher education and the public. This involves government funding of research based on a peer-review process (not government mandates) and relative autonomy for universities to manage their own affairs. In exchange, universities are expected to produce useful knowledge, contribute to the health of the nation, produce human capital for highly skilled positions, and educate students to participate in our democracy as good citizens. The high level of trust that this implies, Berg stated, has broken down over the past decades and is being replaced by an environment of increased demands and regulations in which universities bear an increasing share of the risk for unanticipated problems and unfunded mandates.

Next, Chancellor Grantham discussed a series of little-known and somewhat surprising facts that need to be kept in mind in any conversation about the partnership, though acknowledging that all in the room may not agree about their relative importance. He began by discussing economically disadvantaged students, for whom elite, private universities are often more affordable than publics; only 8 percent of low-income students go to the best college they can be admitted to. He went on to state that academic major is not a predictor of success in obtaining a job on graduation, and less selective colleges are as successful as highly selective ones in producing graduates who are engaged in the workplace. Also, the often criticized tenure system, he said, is in fact an economic advantage for most colleges and universities because of the reduction in costs in recruitment and retention of highly trained professionals. Last, industry has largely gotten out of basic research, so research universities are critical for new medical discoveries; higher education has become the second biggest funder of medical research after the National Institutes of Health.

Speaker Radford then laid out his expectations of the university and made it clear that meeting these expectations was required as a condition of continued state funding. First, state schools must produce graduates who can succeed in the job market. If a college education does not result in a good job, the state is not receiving a satisfactory return on its investment. Second, the university health care system must provide high-quality medical care for citizens of the state as well as support important medical research that will improve lives. Third, the state's universities must be engines of economic growth, creating jobs and tax revenue and improving the quality of life in the communities that surround them. Last, higher education in the state must produce big ideas that can be commercialized by the private sector.

Governor Capps expressed the hope that the discussion will clearly lay out the expectations on all sides and then effectively communicate them to all interested parties. He warned against telling one story to the legislature or the newspapers and another to the faculty and students. He urged all in the room to engage one another and expressly address points of view different from their own.

The Conversation

The conversation began with Student Body President Darien discussing student concerns. First, she discussed a lack of interest in teaching on the part of many faculty, including some of the most distinguished. "They seem to be much more interested in their research than in actually teaching us," she said. She went on to explain that "half her classes were taught by grad students, postdocs, and adjuncts." Speaker Radford responded that this was precisely what his colleagues in the legislature were concerned about. "They want to know what exactly these professors are doing with their time if they aren't teaching students," he said. Professor Stem responded that young tenure-track faculty were under tremendous pressure from their departments to publish research and bring in grants, and their academic futures were dependent on their success in those areas. "No one gets tenure for good teaching," she said. Governor Capps said, "I don't know how you get the incentives aligned, but I can tell you it is indefensible that faculty do not shoulder a full teaching load, and you administrators should teach as well. Everyone should be teaching."

Darien then turned to jobs. "When we come to campus as first-year students, we expect to leave four years later with good jobs. In many cases my fellow students have left good full-time or part-time jobs to pursue a college degree, and they expect a better job than the one they left. We all expect to obtain a degree in four years or less. Unfortunately, the faculty don't seem to have job placement or career readiness as part of their job description." Chancellor Grantham echoed these concerns. "We aren't doing enough to prepare students for their first job. We need to begin this process during the first semester and have a clear methodology for career readiness," he said. "Students and their parents expect this, especially if they are incurring debt that must be paid off after graduation."

Professor Stem strongly objected to this careerist perspective. "A college education should be designed to prepare students for jobs that haven't been invented yet," she said. "If our students learn problem-solving skills and critical thinking and can effectively express themselves orally and in writing, then getting a job will take care of itself. Recent research confirms that study in the liberal arts and sciences is the best preparation for a job and that several years out liberal arts majors do as well or better as students with a more technical or career-oriented degree."

Chairman Nichols quickly responded, "Sylvia, I've heard that answer many times before, and it isn't good enough. Faculty must embrace job readiness as part of their mission and not treat it as something that is carried out by low-level administrators. Our students and their parents expect it, and it is a responsibility we must assume in exchange for the state funding and tuition dollars we receive." Governor Capps commented, "We must pay attention to students. If they are not leaving the university with a valuable degree and a positive experience, we will lose the political capital necessary to maintain a great university experience."

Last, Student Body President Darien addressed the political environment on campus. "Marginalized students don't feel welcome here," she said. "The administration refuses to add spaces and resources to help students deal with the daily microaggressions they have to tolerate from their privileged peers." Speaker Radford jumped in quickly. "These statements just fuel the greatest fears of the legislature," he said. "The talk of safe spaces is what alienates our members the most: it is a direct result of the indoctrination that occurs on the liberal campus, fueled most by the leftist faculty." Governor Capps added that these were problems that the administration needed to figure out how to solve. President Darien agreed.

The conversation next turned to the faculty. Professor Stem commented that the discussion so far was going "just as she expected." The views of students and their parents are important, she said, but "students are not customers who should be catered to, and the value of a liberal education can't be measured solely by lifetime earnings." She reminded the group that faculty salaries had been frozen by the legislature for the past three years, and state-supported schools such as theirs were having a difficult time remaining competitive with private institutions for the best professors. Faculty, she said, are "frustrated by the growth in the administrative bureaucracy and the amount of resources this takes away from teaching and research." She was also critical of efforts aimed at economic development and entrepreneurship, which she characterized as "draining resources from the core mission of the university. The very idea of the university was to create a unique space where intellectual curiosity can be pursued without the need to justify its commercial or societal value."

After a long pause, Chairman Nichols thanked Professor Stem for laying out an important viewpoint that must be understood and made a part of the conversation. Speaker Radford responded that "faculty still don't get it. How am I going to go to my colleagues in the legislature and ask them to support you if the faculty aren't willing to carry a full teaching load, help students get a job, and undertake research that will make our citizens' everyday lives better? In fact, I need more than that. I need to prove there is a return on the taxpayers' investment in job creation and tax revenue. The days of unquestioned support are over, and we have to be able to justify our expenditures to very skeptical voters whose confidence in higher education seems to be diminishing year by year."

Professor Stem stated that the speaker's expectations were never made clear to faculty, and that wasn't "what they signed up for when they came to the university. You hired us and told us to succeed in research. Now you're throwing a huge set of expectations at us after the fact." Chairman Nichols said that was the problem. "There needs to be a more explicit understanding and ultimately an acceptance of the public's expectations combined with a set of initiatives designed to better address them." Chancellor Grantham responded, "This has to be a two-way street. If the university community is to meet these new or at least newly enunciated expectations, the taxpayers must be willing to support the institution at a level that allows it to remain competitive." Governor Capps immediately replied that he agreed but that costs and tuition had gotten out of hand and that the state's colleges and universities must begin making the same tough economic decisions that businesses in the state had been forced to make since the Great Recession. "We've hit a ceiling on the tuition increases that allowed you to ignore economic reality. Now we have to figure out how to gain economies of scale using technology. It seems that the curiosity of our faculty does not extend to the issues of how we make ourselves better and do more with less. Maybe we need to change the reward and recognition structure for the faculty to encourage this."

Chancellor Grantham applauded the "robust discussion" but suggested it was important to put it into context. The university, by virtually any measure, was one of the best in the country. Its research was making a difference in the lives of people all over the world, its faculty included a Nobel Prize winner, and its students consistently won Rhodes scholarships. "The people of our state don't realize what a gem we have. Other states and even most private institutions would love to be in our situation."

"If that is the case," said Governor Capps, "then we need to do a much better job telling our story. But we can't tell the story effectively until we have an explicit understanding of the partnership between the taxpayers and the university. That's going to take some work. We need more conversations like this one involving legislators and faculty members, and we ultimately need to come to some agreement that will provide the needed support to higher education in our state and at the same time restore the trust of our citizens that higher education is a force for good."

Chairman Nichols ended the meeting by thanking all of the attendees. Before he adjourned, Chancellor Grantham jumped in. "This is an important conversation," he said. "For too long, administrators have listened to one audience at a time and tried to solve their problems. That approach won't work anymore. We have too many constituencies with too many diametrically opposed views to think that we can solve any of these problems in isolation. It's going to take keeping every voice at the table. It's going to take listening to all sides. I appreciate the candor and courage that all of you are exhibiting and hope you will stay in this process."

MAKING IT REAL

We chose a public university for our fictional musings, but similar conversations are going on at all sorts of institutions, public and private. In the real conversation, we think that some critical priorities must be kept in mind.

Keep Track of the Promises

The university has taken on so many different expectations that it is no longer viable simply to make promises to one group in a vacuum. New promises to one group often reduce the financial and psychic capital of other constituents. Increasing effort in innovation and entrepreneurship, complying with new federal regulations, satisfying student concerns for programs in identity and counseling, providing robust information technology—all of these somewhat tangential goals take funds away from the core missions of research and teaching. Promises cannot be made in isolation anymore. The university needs to be transparent with all of its stakeholders about all of the sometimes conflicting promises that have been made.

Recognize the need for expertise. Colleges and universities are complex entities, and running them takes deep expertise. At a research university, health care, financial aid, tenure and faculty governance, research compliance, graduate student funding, state and local government—these are all challenging areas that require experience and firsthand knowledge. Because trustees come from outside the institution, they must rely on long-time academic hands in developing a shared understanding. At some institutions this is facilitated by asking individual trustees to develop expertise in discrete areas and share that knowledge with the board at large.

Listen to Outside Voices

We asked Chancellor Folt what she saw as the biggest disconnect in higher education. "I really think it's a misalignment between the elitism of the faculty and human experience," she said. "A lot of people love universities, and the ones who love it the most often got to be friends with individual faculty. But when you go out in other places, they feel that universities and the faculty look down on them. That we don't think they're smart enough, we don't think they understand complexity. They believe and hear—whether it's true or not—what looks to be a barrage of elitism coming from the faculty." There are two sides to this, of course. The public has become more and more resistant to the importance of knowledge and expertise, and this has contributed to the isolation of scholars. But the disconnect is one that can no longer be ignored.

Listen to Student Voices

Today's undergraduates are a source of inspiration. They are idealistic about the world and have many more skills and abilities than their predecessors. Nevertheless, many students are hurting. The ones who seemingly have it made—who come from affluent backgrounds and are attending selective colleges—may be struggling with mental health issues, overly involved parents, substance abuse, isolation fostered by social media, and the pressure of high expectations. The ones who are overcoming other obstacles—low-income students, people of color, LGBTQ students—are struggling with all of this, and more. What is required is deep engagement by faculty and staff with students. "I think that so many of our leaders forget that students are really a constituency that should be understood and should be valued," says Gordon Gee.

Listen to Faculty Voices

It is easy to point to the faculty as isolated and uninterested in the larger problems of the university. "Most of them just want to leave the administration and how universities are run to others," says Jonathan Cole, "and when necessary blame the others for not doing something that they think ought to be done." Though there is truth to this, we believe it results partly from the failure of the administration to enlist the faculty in the right way. They are rewarded mostly for the quantity and quality of their research and very rarely for investment in the overall goals of the institution.

Chris Newfield longs for a system in which "loyalists" would be rewarded and faculty could decide after they got tenure "that what you really love is contributing to the overall benefit of the institution," he says. "You're good at it, you like being on senate committees, and you like being the graduate chair even though that takes hours out of both your teaching and your research. You could get reasonable raises and wouldn't be worried that you were not going to be able to afford college for your kids."

Newfield laments that we do not reward these types of faculty. "The loyalists were punished for being loyalists, and they felt kind of bad and demoralized and unappreciated even though they were the glue that kept the whole thing together and also did good research and really interesting teaching." This debate has raged for decades, but we believe that we cannot prolong the argument any longer. Going to the faculty, asking for help in rebuilding the partnership, and rewarding them for doing so can be a powerful act.

Do Not Forget How Helpful the Staff Can Be

Most folks who work at universities do so because they believe in the mission. Interestingly, in the Gallup-Purdue study, the effectiveness of a mentor was unrelated to whether the mentor was a tenured faculty member or other staff worker.[3] This is a highly empowering idea, and while many staff look at this and roll their eyes, as they know they have been doing this important work for all these years, there is the opportunity to bring the faculty and staff together around mentoring students. Praising the work of the staff in enabling the functions of the university and providing research and teaching is critical.

TELLING THE STORY

We believe that universities have not done enough to tell the story of the important work that goes on within their walls. That's why so many accounts of successful research and expanded access come as a surprise to outside stakeholders. "I think there is a need for us to explain far better than we have, and I put the blame squarely upon the academic community as much as anyone else," says Cole. He laments "the failure to explain to the broader population—whether they be state legislators, governors, senators, representatives, or the educated public—exactly what is lost" when state support to public universities is cut. We need to describe vividly, he says, "how that has an impact on the economic developments of the state, the types of people who live there, the type of people who come there, and the overall way in which it has an adverse effect on the people of the United States and the people of the world because it is going to lower the rate of discovery in a substantial way."

Some of this needs to be done within our own community. "We don't do a very good job actually when the people are with us," says Washington University chancellor Mark Wrighton. "We have college students for four years and then for graduate and professional students, it's quite variable, but they're spending six years with us. The fact that they leave not understanding how to finance higher education, shame on us." Similarly, faculty and staff are not well informed about the costs of research and how funds are used. "We need to spend a little time telling them what that's all about," Wrighton says, "I think that most of our faculty believe that we're making money on research."

Carol Folt gave us an emotional anecdote about all of this. "We were having a lot of conversations about students not necessarily feeling included," she says, "and you could say these were students from all kinds of backgrounds—they could be athletes, they could be conservative students, they could be black students—but they weren't feeling comfortable. One of the faculty members said to me that when he grew up, the rule in his family was that 'if anyone comes into my living room, I'm going to make sure that they feel as welcome and as part of the community as my family. Universities no longer make people feel like they're welcoming them into their living room.' I thought that was a really good embodiment of it. It has to feel like it's theirs, whether they go here or not. So they have to relate to us."

Rebuilding the Partnership

The process of rebuilding the partnership between higher education and the American public is well under way. For the two of us, not a day goes by without a discussion of at least one of the issues raised in this book. More broadly, there has never been more commentary about higher education in the popular press, and policymakers—and even filmmakers—have gravitated to the challenges facing American colleges and universities.

We presume that most of the readers of this book are already or soon will be involved in the rebuilding process in some way and that they will be having conversations on these issues both inside and outside of the academy. We also suspect that our readers would appreciate takeaways that will better equip them to participate in those conversations and the process of managing, growing, and financing colleges and universities of all shapes and sizes. What follows are suggestions specifically directed at members of the various constituencies that make up the university community.

TRUSTEES AND POLICYMAKERS

Do Not Micromanage

Often academic leaders assume their position with much less executive experience than those serving as trustees. Although academic leaders are expected to think like Stephen Hawking and talk like Jack Welch, they usually start off with more of the former. In most cases, these new leaders are a product of the academy with essentially no managerial experience outside a college or university. This imbalance of executive experience can prompt board members to feel that they need to involve themselves in the day-to-day operations of the institution and, in the worst case, introduce management techniques and vocabulary that do not work in a university.[1]

They usually soon realize that academic institutions cannot be managed like corporations, but they may overlook constructive steps that board members can take to support new academic leaders without overstepping the bounds between board and executive. We have found leadership training programs, such as those run by the Center for Creative Leadership or the Harvard School of Education, to be particularly helpful, and many chancellors employ a private coach on a formal or informal basis to provide a sounding board. Outside consultants on strategy, cost management, and government relations may also prove helpful if they have sufficient understanding of the special nature of the university. Peer leadership groups may be the most constructive, in which a new leader meets regularly with others similarly situated to talk through common problems. Such a group is often invaluable in a crisis, when calm voices that are not deeply involved can provide important perspective.

Let Chancellors Appoint Their Own Teams

In many colleges and universities, an infrastructure with close ties to the board sometimes stays in place through multiple administrations. The justification for this is most often the value of "institutional memory" or having staff who "know where the bodies are buried." This shadow administration can take on inordinate power because it has a direct line to the board, undermining the chancellor's ability to lead. Of course, it makes sense for the board to be part of the hiring process and consulted on building and changing the leadership team. In the end, however, after a chancellor has weighed all of the opinions, he or she needs to build the team with the support of the board.

Be Clear That the Chancellor Is a Faculty Member

The leader of a hospital is traditionally a doctor, law firms are led by a lawyer, and—with rare exceptions—universities should be run by academics.[2] The board should understand and support the reality that engaging in the life of the university—including attending lectures, convening discussions, and teaching—is an essential part of the chancellor's job description. As difficult issues arise, expect to hear the comment that the chancellor is too close to the faculty. At excellent universities, the right response is that the chancellor *is* a member of the faculty.

Celebrate Research and Graduate Education

Research is the reason that American higher education is the envy of the world, but for many trustees and policymakers its importance takes a back seat to their enthusiasm for undergraduate education and athletics. Trustees should take an active interest in campus research, it should be highlighted at trustee meetings, and support for graduate students should be high on the funding agenda. Outside research funding adds to the influence of the institution, and state-of-the-art labs and capabilities are the highest priorities for many on the faculty. In our experience, if board members take the time to learn about ongoing research, they inevitably become excited about and often become ardent supporters of not only the research agenda but also the graduate students that make it possible.

Politics Are Everywhere

Whether in the arts and humanities or the professional schools, institutional politics permeate the university, and the issue almost always involves allocation of resources. Trustees often assume that professional schools take a more disciplined approach to running their enterprises, but at bottom the issue is the same: deans and professors want the institution to invest more in their school or department and, assuming finite resources, less in some other part of the university. The squabbling is not confined to money—ask any dean of arts and sciences who proposes to revise the curriculum and eliminate the foreign language requirement. Effective trustees take the time to understand the politics of important internal decisions, just as they do when dealing with external policymakers. Doing so takes time and good listening skills, but it results in better decisions.

PRESIDENTS, CHANCELLORS, AND ADMINISTRATORS

Stay Close to Students

No chancellor ever regretted spending too much time with students, as they are the best ambassadors for the institution, both in the short run, as they talk to their friends and family, and in the long run, as they become permanent members of the alumni community, donors, and policymakers. Notwithstanding conventional wisdom, it is possible for leaders also to teach, especially if a team-teaching arrangement can be structured. Short of teaching a class, guest lectures are easy to arrange, and once faculty know you are available, you will receive more invitations than you can accept. Finally, informal interactions over coffee or lunch can be the most enjoyable. Be visible and available, and you will be amazed how much you can learn and how much goodwill you can generate.

Do Not Forget You Are a Faculty Member

Give talks, spend some time keeping up with your field, and keep a little research going with your collaborators. Consider teaching a course or seminar. Go to academic talks on campus and ask questions. Running a great university gives you license to be interested in everything. The most important trait for an academic leader is to be genuinely curious about your colleagues' research. If you are interested, it will show. Do not let your board split you from the faculty. If they say you are "too close" to the faculty, that's good. Every time you make a decision, ask if you could explain it to yourself as a newly tenured associate professor. That is still you.

Be Suspicious of Administration

Administration is a necessary evil at best. The university has to be operated—students have to be admitted, they need a place to live, faculty searches have to be done, and so on. But none of that is the true work of the university, which is done by students and faculty. Do not forget that you are overhead; every time you spend money, ask yourself whether that money would be better spent hiring a new tenure-track faculty member or going to financial aid. If you meet someone who says, "Sorry I didn't know you were the provost/dean/chancellor," tell them that that's great because it means you are doing your job. If they know who you are, it's usually not good.

Engage with Academic Medicine

If you are a chancellor or provost and do not come from academic medicine, you need to learn as much as you can about the medical school and the hospital. Get a lab coat and a badge and start walking around as if you are in charge. Ask if you can go on rounds or shadow in the emergency room. Study the books carefully. For many, health care is a big part of the budget. Moreover, lives are at stake.

Raise Funds for True Priorities

In university fundraising, the hardest thing is to say no. Your development director always wants to take every gift, but many gifts will cost you money. The chancellor is the only person who can decide not to take one; we know a chancellor who turned down the gift of a large estate because the donor insisted that it could not be sold and there was no accompanying endowment to maintain it. Every gift seems too small ten years later, so do not get hypnotized by the size of the original gift. Directing the fundraising to the right priorities is by far the best way to influence the future of the institution.

Reunite the Graduate and Undergraduate Universities

All research institutions are gradually breaking in two: one university with tenured and tenure-track faculty that trains graduate students and does research; and another that does undergraduate education, with much of the teaching being done by student affairs staff, part-time faculty, lecturers, and graduate students. Many of the biggest challenges facing higher education are a result of this growing disconnect, which will not be resolved until the two universities are reunited. All faculty must teach. Research must be interpreted in a way that clearly demonstrates its value to society. All of this is central to the partnership with the public.

FACULTY

Teach

Tenured and tenure-track faculty get rewarded and promoted based on research, and running a lab, teaching graduate seminars, and publishing one's research are the keys to success. But the rise of an administrative university that solely teaches undergraduates is partly the fault of faculty prioritizing their research and allowing undergraduate education to be outsourced. Take it back. Teach undergraduate courses with enthusiasm, and do not let department chairs and other administrators take those courses from you. In the current system, you will not be rewarded directly for doing this, but you and your discipline will continue to get penalized in multiple ways if the faculty doesn't reclaim undergraduate education. In the long run, faculty incentives must be reimagined to reflect this teaching imperative.

Participate in the Community

Be visible on campus and in your department, and be wary of taking too many leaves. Explaining why faculty are not teaching or are not in the building to an outsider is essentially impossible. If you are worried about the defunding of the university, make it easier on your chancellor and board by being completely engaged in the community.

Understand the Job Prospects of Your Graduate Students

The growth of the adjunct faculty and the marginalization of graduate education are being driven in part by the poor job prospects for graduate students in many fields. The solution to this is to be thoughtful about how many graduate students are admitted and make sure they know in advance the reality of their job prospects. It is very common for former graduate students who are stuck in positions outside of their field to say that they were told when they applied to graduate school that they would be tenure-track professors one day, and they feel cheated when they find out how slim the chances of that are.

Understand How Your Department Is Staffing Its Classes

Causes of the low wages and poor working conditions for adjunct faculty and graduate students are many, but one of them is that they're needed to cover classes for tenure-track faculty who are on research leaves or teaching graduate seminars. If the supply of adjunct labor is high, it drives down wages. Administration needs to help counteract this, but the tenure-track faculty need to understand and own the problem, too. We have found that when adjunct or fixed-term faculty push for better benefits or to form unions, it often emerges that the tenured and tenure-track faculty were unaware of their colleagues' situation. It will take collaboration between the administration and the tenured faculty to solve these problems.

Do Not Ask for New Administration

Ironically, the unsustainable growth in administrative personnel is often driven by influential faculty who request a high-level administrator for their program while at the same time bemoaning the growth in administration at the expense of teaching and research. A faculty star told us that the only way his legacy could be preserved was to create a new vice chancellor whose job is to further the interests of his multidisciplinary curriculum and research. A better approach, we suggested, was for this beloved professor to raise an endowment for his program before his retirement.

STUDENTS

Do Your Homework before Applying

The vast amount of information available to prospective students, the complex set of options for financing higher education, and the increased diversity of those considering higher education make it more important than ever that prospective students do their homework. If a college is to have any chance of meeting an incoming student's expectations, the fit between what the student is seeking and what the school has to offer must be strong. Aside from the content of the curriculum, applicants should assess the campus environment using data available online and supplement that data with conversations with current and former students to get a full picture of campus life.

Join the Community

Colleges and universities are communities designed for the pursuit of learning. Much of that learning takes place outside the classroom, in public lectures, laboratories, concerts, art exhibits, and theater performances. But only a small proportion of undergraduates participate in any of these activities unless they are required to do so for a class.

As a start, live on campus for at least a year or two if circumstances permit. Aside from the intrinsic value of exposure to a community that values the life of the mind (such exposure is not routinely available after graduation), being active in the campus community increases the likelihood of achieving your goals after graduation. Simply showing up for class for four years and getting a passing grade confers no great advantage. If you expect to receive the full value of that diploma, you have to meet your school halfway by participating in the community you have been selected to join. Being part of the community also involves the opportunity to do research and participate in the discovery of new knowledge. This is a once-in-a-lifetime opportunity.

Students also have an important role to play in the ongoing dialogue about the university's partnership with the public. Student perspectives are critical to the discussion of both specific campus issues and the national challenges facing higher education.

Clarify Your Goals

Once you have been accepted to college and have joined the community, be clear about your expectations, and structure your time and your course work accordingly. If you are a traditional college student just out of high school and not sure what you want to do in life, college is a great place to explore and it makes sense to sample a broad range of courses and activities. It may well turn out that the job or vocation you are interested in when you graduate had not been invented when you began school.

On the other hand, if you are a single mom who is returning to school in order to get a better job, your choices could be more limited, and you will likely be balancing family obligations with the demands of obtaining a degree and perhaps even part-time work. This presents a very different calculus in which mixing online courses and perhaps evening classes in an effort to finish school in as short a period as possible will make the most sense.

The point is that obtaining a useful, meaningful, and valuable education is a two-way street. To get what you want and need from your college experience, you must have goals and objectives even if they change several times during the process.

Ask for Help

College is designed to be a challenging experience, and few students obtain a degree without help. Do not be reluctant to ask. If you are worried about getting a job, start getting ready as early as your first year by talking to career services or seeking out internships. Ask around about informal contacts as well. Professors and fellow students involved in interesting enterprises and projects are a great source of leads for internships and other experiences that will help with job readiness when you graduate. Also, stay in touch with academic advising to be sure you stay on track for graduation. Graduating late or not at all—possibly the worst result of a college experience—can often be avoided if you pay attention to your adviser. Rely on your parents for emotional support, but take responsibility for your own education, including being ready for life after graduation.

Graduate Students Have Unique Challenges

It is getting harder and harder to obtain a berth as a tenure-track professor, for reasons we have discussed previously, so the traditional academic track is not a realistic career goal for most graduate students. Graduate students still have futures in the research enterprise, but success should not be measured by whether one finds lifelong employment in academia. Be realistic about your job prospects, be open to work in the private sector and so-called nontraditional jobs, and finish as quickly as you can. Research is hard, and doing something truly original is one of the most challenging tasks in the world. It cannot be rushed, but getting finished sooner is good for everyone when it can be done.

As we pursue our own conversations toward rebuilding the partnership, three things are clear to us. First, it is a gift, a *higher calling*, to be part of American higher education and thereby a part of the important conversation about rebuilding the partnership. Second, because the partnership is with the public, all must be invited to join in the conversation. Of course, we expect faculty, students, administrators, trustees, and policymakers to be deeply involved in the debate about the issues we raise, but we hope the discussion will involve many others. As one faculty member said, "If students are not strictly customers, then who is our customer?" The answer is the American public: virtually every American has a direct or indirect stake in our system of higher education. Third, and most important, it is critical to the national interest that American higher education grow and flourish in the face of the obstacles it is now facing. There is no more important manifestation of American ideals, there is no set of institutions more successful at discovering new knowledge, and there is no comparable force better positioned to tackle the world's biggest problems.

Acknowledgments

Every book is a team effort. Our books start with two authors that have different native languages. One of us is a career academic who insists on Oxford commas, "data are," and words like "epistemology" and "concomitant"; the other started out in the business world and uses phrases like "data-driven" and "the train has left the station." The process of finding a common language is much like the struggle between the academy and the public that lies at the heart of this book. So, collaboration is the centerpiece not just of the book but of how it was written.

It wasn't until we talked to a collection of university trustees that we developed an understanding of the foundational ideas that drove our work on the book. These trustees articulated a hunger for more information about how the university works and a willingness to dig into the details. At the same time, they expressed a belief that colleges and universities must do more to meet their expectations. For these initial interviews, we thank Tom Hillman, Gene Kahn, Maxine Clark, Lowry Caudill, Sallie Shuping-Russell, and Julia Grumbles.

We especially thank MIT trustee Desh Deshpande for strong guidance during this early phase of our work and for hosting a dinner of college leaders that dramatically influenced our thinking.

A diverse set of voices from inside and outside the academy added nuance and a hard dose of reality to our thinking. This group includes: Joel Fleishman, Chris Newfield, Michael Lomax, Carol Folt, Mark Wrighton, Gordon Gee, Sanjay Sarma, Phil Clay, Jeff Selingo, Troy Hammond, and Goldie Blumenstyk. Their views appear throughout the text. Of special note is Jonathan Cole, who inspires us both with his writing and with his encouragement. His ideas are at the heart of our belief that repairing the long-standing but generally unrecognized partnership between America and its colleges and universities is the key task before us.

There are those who read the manuscript and gave us helpful feedback. In addition to many of those mentioned above, we are grateful to Craig Schnuck, Jay Schalin, Mary Sue Coleman, John McGowan, Kevin Guskiewicz, Erin Schuettpelz, and Matthew Raskoff. We also received ongoing feedback from our students and colleagues at Washington University and the University of North Carolina.

Both of our books have benefited from a strong partnership with David Perry, and we are grateful to him for coming out of retirement long enough to help us with the manuscript.

Mark Simpson-Vos, Jay Mazzocchi, and the folks at UNC Press did their usual great job in getting the manuscript reviewed, revised, and printed.

The book would not have been possible without the scholarly and expert assistance of Dr. Ashley Macrander, who provided invaluable research assistance and continuous and important feedback. Lisa Siddens provided extremely useful technical assistance as the manuscript was prepared.

The Highland Vineyard Foundation and Washington University provided financial support to make all of this possible. All of the authors' royalties will be contributed to a fund designed to promote the ideas in the book and the conversation we hope it encourages. We especially appreciate the encouragement and support we received from Mark Wrighton and for allowing the work on the book to be based at Washington University.

Finally, we are eternally grateful to Patti Thorp and Kay Goldstein for their love and support. From the very beginning, they have made our collaboration possible in ways both known and unknown to the two of us.

Notes

All Web addresses are accurate as of December 2017.

ABBREVIATIONS

CHE   *Chronicle of Higher Education*
IHE   *Inside Higher Ed*
NYT   *New York Times*
USNWR   *U.S. News & World Report*
WP   *Washington Post*
WSJ   *Wall Street Journal*

INTRODUCTION

1. Since the publication of *Engines of Innovation*, one of us has moved from a university where he established an innovation initiative to another university where "enabling innovation and entrepreneurship" was already one of the four pillars of the fundraising campaign.

2. The clinical departments in medical schools are somewhat more like businesses than other parts of the university.

3. A. A. Smith, "Apollo Sale Approved, with Conditions," *IHE*, December 8, 2016, retrieved from https://www.insidehighered.com/news/2016/12/08/education-department-approves-apollo-deal-conditions.

4. A. Bidwell, "For-Profit Corinthian Colleges Filed for Chapter 11 Bankruptcy," *USNWR*, May 4, 2015, retrieved from http://www.usnews.com/news/articles/2015/05/04/for-profit-corinthian-colleges-files-for-chapter-11-bankruptcy.

5. J. Christie, "ITT Educational Services Filed for Bankruptcy to Start Liquidation," *Reuters*, September 16, 2016, retrieved from http://in.reuters.com/article/itt-education-bankruptcy-idINL2N1BT02R.

6. The Purdue faculty are opposing this transaction, and how this will all play out remains to be determined. R. Seltzer, "Purdue Faculty Questions Kaplan Deal," *IHE*, May 5, 2017, retrieved from https://www.insidehighered.com/news/2017/05/05/purdue-faculty-votes-against-kaplan-process.

7. Y. Joseph and M. McPhate, "Mount St. Mary's President Quits after Firings Seen as Retaliatory," *NYT*, February 29, 2016, retrieved from http://www.nytimes.com/2016/03/02/us/simon-newman-resigns-as-president-of-mount-st-marys.html?_r=0.

8. J. R. Cole, *Toward a More Perfect University* (New York: Public Affairs, 2016).

9. Ibid., 11–12.

10. J. Mitchell and D. Belkin, "Americans Losing Faith in College Degrees, Poll Finds," *WSJ*, September 7, 2017, retrieved from https://www.wsj.com/articles/americans-losing-faith-in-college-degrees-poll-finds-1504776601.

11. A. B. Giamatti, *A Free and Ordered Space: The Real World of the University* (New York: W. W. Norton, 1988), 17.

12. E. Lutz and L. Kennedy, "Today's College Students Infographic," *Bill & Melinda Gates Foundation*, 2015, retrieved from http://postsecondary .gatesfoundation.org/areas-of-focus/incentives/policy-advocacy/advocacy-priorities/america-100-college-students/.

13. E. Sherman, "Wealthy Kids 8 Times More Likely to Graduate College Than Poor," *Forbes*, February, 5, 2015, retrieved from https://www.forbes.com/sites/eriksherman/2015/02/05/wealthy-college-kids-8-times-more-likely-to-graduate-than-poor/#3f55866fdfb.

CHAPTER 1

1. Times Higher Education, "World University Rankings,"2018, retrieved from https://www.timeshighereducation.com/world-university-rankings/2018/world-ranking#!/page/0/length/25/sort_by/rank/sort_order/asc/cols/stats.

2. D. F. Labaree, *A Perfect Mess: The Unlikely Ascendancy of American Higher Education* (Chicago: University of Chicago Press, 2017).

3. "Criminology and Criminal Justice Major," Eastern Michigan University catalog, 2017, retrieved from http://catalog.emich.edu/preview_program .php?catoid=20&poid=10110&returnto=3608.

4. N. Anderson, "A History Degree without Studying U.S. History? It's Possible at Top Colleges like Harvard, Yale, and Stanford," *WP*, July 7, 2016, retrieved from https://www.washingtonpost.com/news/grade-point/wp/2016/07/07/a-history-degree-without-studying-u-s-history-its-possible -at-these-top-colleges/.

5. K. Kiley, "Another Liberal Arts Critic," *IHE*, January 30, 2013, retrieved from https://www.insidehighered.com/news/2013/01/30/north-carolina-governor-joins-chorus-republicans-critical-liberal-arts.

6. N. Waller, "Hunting for Soft Skills, Companies Scoop Up English Majors," *WSJ*, October 25, 2016, retrieved from http://www.wsj.com/articles/hunting-for-soft-skills-companies-scoop-up-english-majors-1477404061.

7. C. Straumsheim, "Decision Time," *IHE*, August 24, 2016, retrieved from https://www.insidehighered.com/news/2016/08/24/study-finds-students-benefit-waiting-declare-major.

8. M. C. Nussbaum, *Not for Profit: Why Democracy Needs the Humanities* (Princeton, N.J.: Princeton University Press, 2010).

9. S. Jaschik, "Making the Case for Liberal Arts Colleges," *IHE*, January 9, 2017, retrieved from https://www.insidehighered.com/news/2017/01/09/research-documents-life-impact-attending-liberal-arts-college.

10. V. Bush, *Science: The Endless Frontier*, 1945, retrieved from https://www.nsf.gov/od/lpa/nsf50/vbush1945.htm.

11. J. R. Cole, *The Great American University: Its Rise to Preeminence, Its Indispensable National Role, Why It Must Be Protected* (New York: Public Affairs, 2009).

12. National Cancer Institute, "Cancer Moonshot," 2017, retrieved from https://www.cancer.gov/research/key-initiatives/moonshot-cancer-initiative; National Institutes of Health, "What Is the BRAIN Initiative?," 2017, retrieved from https://www.braininitiative.nih.gov.

13. Cole, *Great American University*, 85–108.

14. E. Cornell to A. D. White, February 23, 1868, retrieved from http://rmc.library.cornell.edu/ezra/exhibition/anystudy/.

15. Cole, *Great American University*, 64.

16. L. Menand, "The Limits of Academic Freedom," in *The Future of Academic Freedom*, ed. L. Menand (Chicago: University of Chicago Press, 1996), 4.

17. Cole, *Great American University*, 384.

18. https://freeexpression.uchicago.edu/page/statement-principles-free-expression.

19. https://source.wustl.edu/2016/09/washington-university-affirms-commitment-freedom-expression/).

20. Cole, *Great American University*, 53.

CHAPTER 2

1. B. Wermund, "University Presidents: We've Been Blindsided," *Politico*, December 19, 2017, retrieved from https://www.politico.com/story/2017/12/19/college-university-backlash-elitism-296898.

2. Business Wire, "Undergraduate Enrollments Down 224,000 in Fall 2017: 63,000 Fewer Students Entered College Compared to Previous Fall," December 20, 2017, retrieved from https://www.businesswire.com/news/home/20171220005059/en/Undergraduate-Enrollments-224000-Fall-2017.

3. Wermund, "University Presidents."

4. H. Fingerhut, "Republicans Skeptical of Colleges' Impact on U.S., but Most See Benefits for Workforce Preparation," *Pew Research Center*, July 20, 2017, retrieved from http://www.pewresearch.org/fact-tank/2017/07/20/republicans-skeptical-of-colleges-impact-on-u-s-but-most-see-benefits-for-workforce-preparation/.

5. Wermund, "University Presidents."

6. Q. Bui, "The One Question Most Americans Get Wrong about College Graduates," *NYT*, June 3, 2016, retrieved from https://www.nytimes.com/interactive/2016/06/03/upshot/up-college-unemployment-quiz.html.

7. S. Dynarski, "An Economist's Perspective on Student Loans in the United States," *Brookings Institution*, September 2014, retrieved from https://www.brookings.edu/wp-content/uploads/2016/06/economist_perspective_student_loans_dynarski.pdf.

8. M. Woodruff, "An Ivy League Education Can Be Surprisingly Cheap," *Business Insider*, August 27, 2013, retrieved from http://www.businessinsider.com/ivy-league-schools-are-surprisingly-cheap-net-tuition-2013-8.

9. C. R. Tamborini, C. Kim, and A. Sakamoto, "Education and Lifetime Earnings in the United States," *Demography* 52, no. 4 (2015): 1383–407.

10. D. Belkin, "More Colleges Dropping Out," *WSJ*, July 19, 2017, retrieved from https://www.wsj.com/articles/more-colleges-dropping-out-1500506002.

11. W. Zumeta et al., *Financing American Higher Education in the Era of Globalization* (Cambridge, Mass.: Harvard Education Press, 2012), 8.

12. Ibid., 11.

13. Ibid., 13.

14. E. Lutz and L. Kennedy, "Today's College Students Infographic," *Bill & Melinda Gates Foundation*, 2015, retrieved from http://postsecondary.gatesfoundation.org/areas-of-focus/incentives/policy-advocacy/advocacy-priorities/america-100-college-students/.

15. Zumeta et al., *Financing American Higher Education*, 4.

16. J. J. Selingo, *College (Un)bound: The Future of Higher Education and What It Means for Students* (Las Vegas, Nev.: Amazon, 2013), 62.

17. J. Denneen and T. Dretler, "The Financially Sustainable University," *Bain & Company*, July 6, 2012, retrieved from http://www.bain.com/publications/articles/financially-sustainable-university.aspx.

18. B. Boyington, "See 20 Years of Tuition Growth at National Universities," *USNWR*, September 20, 2017, retrieved from https://www.usnews.com/education/best-colleges/paying-for-college/articles/2017-09-20/see-20-years-of-tuition-growth-at-national-universities.

19. J. Lorin and M. Z. Braun, "College Endowments Seen Posting Worst Returns since 2009," *Bloomberg*, August 2, 2016, retrieved from https://www.bloomberg.com/news/articles/2016-08-02/u-s-college-endowments-seen-posting-worst-returns-since-2009.

20. Harvard University, "Financial Aid Leads to a Record Applicant Pool at Harvard College," *Harvard Gazette*, February 5, 2009, retrieved from http://news.harvard.edu/gazette/story/2009/02/financial-aid-leads-to-a-record-applicant-pool-at-harvard-college/.

21. Selingo, *College (Un)bound*, 60.

22. Ibid.

23. Zumeta et al., *Financing American Higher Education*, 6.

24. Selingo, *College (Un)bound*, 63.

25. Ibid., 63.

26. Ibid., 61.

27. Moody's, "Moody's: U.S. Higher Education Outlook Revised to Stable as Revenues Stabilize," July 20, 2015, retrieved from https://www.moodys.com/research/Moodys-US-higher-education-outlook-revised-to-stable-as-revenues—PR_330530.

28. Denneen and Dretler, "Financially Sustainable University."

29. P. Hinrichs, "Trends in Employment at U.S. Colleges and Universities, 1987–2013," *Federal Reserve Bank of Cleveland*, June 13, 2016, retrieved from https://www.clevelandfed.org/newsroom-and-events/publications/economic-commentary/2016-economic-commentaries/ec-201605-trends-in-employment-at-us-colleges-and-universities.aspx.

30. It is not uncommon that some small private colleges do not have a single full-pay student.

31. C. Hoxby and C. Avery, "The Missing 'One-Offs': The Hidden Supply of High-Achieving, Low-Income Students," *Brookings Institution*, Spring 2013, retrieved from https://www.brookings.edu/bpea-articles/the-missing-one-offs-the-hidden-supply-of-high-achieving-low-income-students/.

32. S. Dynarski, "Laptops Are Great, but Not during a Lecture or Meeting," *NYT*, November 22, 2017, retrieved from https://www.nytimes.com/2017/11/22/business/laptops-not-during-lecture-or-meeting.html.

33. Selingo, *College (Un)bound*, 90.

34. The authors created a MOOC on Coursera called "What's Your Big Idea" that has had as many as forty thousand students.

35. Selingo, *College (Un)bound*, 109.

36. D. Bok, *The Struggle to Reform Our Colleges* (Princeton, N.J.: Princeton University Press, 2017).

37. W. J. Baumol and R. Towse, eds., *Baumol's Cost Disease: The Arts and Other Victims* (Cheltenham, U.K.: Edward Elgar, 1997).

38. Selingo, *College (Un)bound*, 97.

39. D. Douglas-Gabriel, "This Chart Tells a Fascinating Story about Higher Education," *WP*, June 8, 2016, retrieved from https://www.washingtonpost.com/news/grade-point/wp/2016/06/08/this-chart-tells-a-fascinating-story-about-higher-education/.

40. Zumeta et al., *Financing American Higher Education*, 111.

41. S. Eddy and K. A. Hogan, "Getting under the Hood: How and for Whom Does Increasing Course Structure Work?," *CBE–Life Sciences Education* 13, no. 3 (2014): 453–68.

42. Selingo, *College (Un)bound*, 84–85.

43. Ibid., 96.

44. Ibid., 79–81.

45. National Association of Colleges and Employers, "Percentage of Students with Internship Experience Climbs," 2015, retrieved from http://www.naceweb.org/s10072015/internship-co-op-student-survey.aspx.

46. P. Hanlon, "Address to the General Faculty," *Dartmouth University*, November 4, 2013, retrieved from http://www.dartmouth.edu/~president/announcements/2013-1104.html.

47. *Starving the Beast: The Battle to Disrupt and Reform America's Public Universities*, written and directed Steve Mims, produced by Bill Banowsky (Violet Crown Films, 2016).

48. P. Hinrichs, "Trends in Employment at U.S. Colleges and Universities, 1987–2013," *Federal Reserve Bank of Cleveland*, June 13, 2016, retrieved from https://www.clevelandfed.org/newsroom-and-events/publications/economic-commentary/2016-economic-commentaries/ec-201605-trends-in-employment-at-us-colleges-and-universities.aspx.

49. Denneen and Dretler, "Financially Sustainable University."

50. B. Sechler, "Ohio State University Trustees Approve 50-Year Parking Lease," *WSJ*, June 22, 2012, retrieved from http://www.wsj.com/articles/SB10001424052702304441404577483010407374878.

CHAPTER 3

1. J. Collins, *Good to Great: Why Some Companies Make the Leap . . . and Others Don't* (New York: HarperCollins, 2001).

2. Much of our thinking on strategy has been influenced by the work of Michael Porter, especially his seminal article, "What Is Strategy?" (*Harvard Business Review* 74, no. 6 [November–December 1996]: 61–78).

3. S. Pearlstein, "Four Tough Things Universities Should Do to Rein in Costs," *WP*, November 25, 2015, retrieved from https://www.washingtonpost.com/opinions/four-tough-things-universities-should-do-to-rein-in-costs/2015/11/25/64fed3de-92c0-11e5-a2d6-f57908580b1f_story.html.

4. It should be noted that these gains have come with a loss in socioeconomic diversity. D. Halikias and R. V. Reeves, "Ladders, Labs, or Laggards? Which Public Universities Contribute Most," *Brookings Institution*, July 11, 2017, retrieved from https://www.brookings.edu/research/ladders-labs-or-laggards-which-public-universities-contribute-most/.

5. T. Kingkade, "California Universities Use Out-of-State Students to Plug Budget Hole, following National Trend," *Huffington Post*, September 13, 2012, retrieved from http://www.huffingtonpost.com/2012/09/12/california-nonresident-enrollment-budget-cuts_n_1859840.html.

6. R. Seltzer, "Black Colleges Dropped from Bill They Opposed," *IHE*, June 6, 2016, retrieved from https://www.insidehighered.com/news/2016/06/06/hbcus-cut-north-carolina-500-tuition-bill.

7. C. Flaherty, "Years of Work, Tabled," *IHE*, April 26, 2017, retrieved from https://www.insidehighered.com/news/2017/04/26/duke-undergraduate-curricular-reform-vote-tabled-indefinitely-after-years-work.

8. M. M. Crow and W. B. Dabars, *Designing the New American University* (Baltimore: Johns Hopkins University Press, 2015), 126.

9. D. Lederman and R. Seltzer, "The Rose-Colored Glasses Come Off: A Survey of Business Officers," *IHE*, July 28, 2017, retrieved from https://www.insidehighered.com/news/survey/rose-colored-glasses-come-survey-business-officers.

10. Ibid.

11. S. Jaschik, "The Disappearing Humanities Jobs," *IHE*, June 6, 2016, retrieved from https://www.insidehighered.com/news/2016/06/06/new-study-documents-long-term-losses-new-humanities-faculty-jobs.

12. M. M. Crow, "New American University: Toward 2025 and Beyond," *Arizona State University*, 2017, retrieved from https://president.asu.edu/about/asucharter.

13. J. Wilson, pers. comm., June 2016.

14. University of Massachusetts, "President Marty Meehan," 2017, retrieved from http://www.massachusetts.edu/about-umass-system/president-marty-meehan.

15. M. Gladwell, "Food Fight," *Revisionist History*, July 14, 2016, retrieved from http://revisionisthistory.com/episodes/05-food-fight.

16. "Economic Diversity among the Top 25 Ranked Schools," *USNWR*, 2017, retrieved from https://www.usnews.com/best-colleges/rankings/national-liberal-arts-colleges/economic-diversity-among-top-ranked-schools.

17. K. Kapsidelis, "One Year Later at Sweet Briar, Counting Success," *Richmond Times-Dispatch*, July 10, 2016, retrieved from http://www.richmond.com/news/virginia/article_43bf1fb9-fecc-5011-873c-315a1abb9da9.html.

18. More on discount rates and financial aid in chapter 4.

19. Sweet Briar College, "Fact Sheet 2016–17," January 9, 2017, retrieved from http://sbc.edu/institutional-effectiveness/wp-content/uploads/sites/16/sbc-fact-sheet-2016-2017.pdf.

20. S. Sickels Locke, "Saving Sweet Briar," *Council for Advancement and Support of Education Currents* 41, no. 9 (2015): 20–27.

21. Ibid.

22. Crow and Dabars, *Designing the New American University*, 18–19.

23. Ibid., 60.

24. D. Von Drehle, "The 10 Best College Presidents," *Time*, November 11, 2009, retrieved from http://content.time.com/time/specials/packages/article/0,28804,1937938_1937934_1937914,00.html.

25. A. A. Arnett, "Education Spotlight: ASU President Michael Crow on Innovation, Tenure and Meeting Demands," *Education Dive*, May 13, 2016, retrieved from http://www.educationdive.com/news/eduvation-spotlight-asu-president-michael-crow-on-innovation-tenure-and-m/418153/.

26. M. M. Crow, "New American University: Toward 2025 and Beyond," *Arizona State University*, 2017, retrieved from https://president.asu.edu/about/asucharter.

27. J. Warner, "ASU Is the 'New American University'—It's Terrifying," *IHE*, January 25, 2015, retrieved from https://www.insidehighered.com/blogs/just-visiting/asu-new-american-university-its-terrifying.

CHAPTER 4

1. General Assembly of the State of North-Carolina, *Act Establishing the University of North Carolina, 1789* (Laws of North-Carolina, 1789), 14–16, retrieved from http://docsouth.unc.edu/unc/unc01-08/unc01-08.html.

2. For this chapter and most of the book, we are focused on undergraduate students. Many important issues surrounding graduate education are discussed elsewhere in detail.

3. L. M. Miranda, vocalist, "My Shot," track 3 of *Hamilton: An American Musical (Original Broadway Cast Recording)*, by L. M. Miranda, L. Odom Jr., A. Ramos, D. Diggs, and O. Onaodowan (New York: Atlantic Records, 2015), 2 compact discs.

4. *John Adams*, written by K. Ellis, directed by T. Hooper, produced by D. Coatsworth and K. Ellis, aired March 16–April 27, 2008, on HBO (New York: HBO Films, 2008).

5. B. Casselman, "Shut Up about Harvard," *FiveThirtyEight*, March 30, 2016, retrieved from https://fivethirtyeight.com/features/shut-up-about-harvard/.

6. Ibid.

7. F. Bruni, *Where You Go Is Not Who You'll Be: An Antidote to the College Admissions Mania* (New York: Hachette Book Group, 2016).

8. R. Chetty et al., "Mobility Report Cards: The Role of Colleges in Intergenerational Mobility," *The Equality of Opportunity Project*, July 2017, retrieved from http://www.equality-of-opportunity.org/papers/coll_mrc_paper.pdf.

9. C. S. Lewis, "Learning in Wartime," *C. S. Lewis Institute*, 1939, retrieved from http://www.cslewisinstitute.org/node/50.

10. C. Hoxby and C. Avery, "The Missing 'One-Offs': The Hidden Supply of High-Achieving, Low-Income Students," *Brookings Institution*, Spring 2013,

retrieved from https://www.brookings.edu/bpea-articles/the-missing-one
-offs-the-hidden-supply-of-high-achieving-low-income-students/.

11. E. Hoover and S. Lipka, "Enrollment Goals Remain Elusive for Small Colleges," *CHE*, December 11, 2016, retrieved from http://www.chronicle.com/article/Enrollment-Goals-Remain/238624.

12. Bureau of Labor Statistics, "Employment Projections," *U.S. Department of Labor*, 2016, retrieved from https://www.bls.gov/emp/ep_chart_001.htm.

13. T. Kroeger, T. Cooke, and E. Gould, "The Class of 2016," *Economic Policy Institute*, April 21, 2016, retrieved from http://www.epi.org/publication/class-of-2016/.

14. Pew Research Center, "The Rising Cost of Not Going to College," February 11, 2014, retrieved from http://www.pewsocialtrends.org/2014/02/11/the-rising-cost-of-not-going-to-college/.

15. Some critics have labeled this problem "credential inflation," noting that having the resources to obtain a college degree is now a gatekeeper to entering the workforce and exacerbates inequality. R. Collins, "Millennials, Rise Up! College Is a Scam—You Have Nothing to Lose but Student Debt," *Salon*, November 24, 2013, retrieved from http://www.salon.com/2013/11/24/millennials_rise_up_college_is_a_scam_you_have_nothing_to_lose_but_student_debt/.

16. D. L. Bennett, A. R. Lucchesi, and R. K. Vedder, "For-Profit Higher Education: Growth, Innovation and Regulation," *Center for College Affordability and Productivity*, July 2010, retrieved from http://files.eric.ed.gov/fulltext/ED536282.pdf.

17. P. Fain, "Full Sail in the Spotlight," *IHE*, January 24, 2012, retrieved from https://www.insidehighered.com/news/2012/01/24/romney-right-about-full-sail-university.

18. J. Puzzanghera, C. Kirkham, and A. Zarembo, "Pentagon Bars University of Phoenix from Recruiting on Military Bases," *Los Angeles Times*, October 9, 2015, retrieved from http://www.latimes.com/business/la-fi-university-of-phoenix-military-20151009-story.html.

19. V. Strauss, "Largest For-Profit U.S. University Expects to Be Put on Probation by Accreditor," *WP*, February 26, 2013, retrieved from https://www.washingtonpost.com/news/answer-sheet/wp/2013/02/26/largest-for-profit-u-s-university-expects-to-be-put-on-probation-by-accreditor/.

20. J. R. Cole, *Toward a More Perfect University* (New York: Public Affairs, 2016).

21. It is important to remember that the Morrill Act predated the birth of external research grants, which were originally given by the Carnegie Foundation decades later. Ibid.

22. Morrill Act of 1862, 7 U.S.C. § 301 (1862).

23. K. W. Olson, "The G.I. Bill and Higher Education: Success and Surprise," *American Quarterly* 25, no. 5 (1973): 596–610.

24. B. Casselman, "The Cost of Dropping Out," *WSJ*, November 22, 2012, retrieved from https://www.wsj.com/articles/SB1000142412788732459590457811 17400943472068.

25. National Center for Education Statistics, "Undergraduate Retention and Graduation Rates," last updated April 2017, retrieved from https://nces.ed.gov/programs/coe/indicator_ctr.asp.

26. CollegeBoard, "Tuition and Fees and Room and Board over Time," 2017, retrieved from https://trends.collegeboard.org/college-pricing/figures-tables/tuition-fees-room-and-board-over-time.

27. D. Leonhardt, "The Assault on Colleges—and the American Dream," *NYT*, May 25, 2017, retrieved from https://www.nytimes.com/2017/05/25/opinion/sunday/the-assault-on-colleges-and-the-american-dream.html.

28. In North Carolina, the system board has always imposed a strict cap of 18 percent on out-of-state students, and California has now been pressuring the prestigious University of California schools to lower their out-of-state enrollments. D. Chemtob, "Out-of-State Enrollment Grows out of North Carolina," *Daily Tar Heel*, February 10, 2016, retrieved from http://www.dailytarheel.com/article/2016/02/out-of-state-enrollment-grows-out-of-north-carolina; R. Rivard, "The New Normal at Berkeley," *IHE*, January 23, 2015, retrieved from https://www.insidehighered.com/news/2015/01/23/gov-brown-says-normal-californians-cant-get-berkeley-problem-some-californians-blame.

29. A valid criticism of the high-tuition–high-aid model is that it squeezes out middle-income students even though these students are often best served by their in-state public universities.

30. The College Solution, "How Much Parents and Students Are Borrowing for College," July 7, 2015, retrieved from http://www.thecollegesolution.com/how-much-parents-and-students-are-borrowing-for-college/.

31. For a full discussion of arithmetic associated with college debt, see The Hechinger Report, "Heaviest Debt Burdens Fall on 3 Types of Students," *USNWR*, June 8, 2015, retrieved from http://www.usnews.com/news/articles/2015/06/08/heaviest-college-debt-burdens-fall-on-3-types-of-students.

32. U.S. Department of Education, "Cohort Default Rate Continues to Drop across All Higher Ed Sectors," September 30, 2015, retrieved from https://www.ed.gov/news/press-releases/cohort-default-rate-continues-drop-across-all-higher-ed-sectors.

33. L. Gelobter, "Under the Hood: Building a New College Scorecard with Students," *The White House*, September 12, 2015, retrieved from https://obamawhitehouse.archives.gov/blog/2015/09/12/under-hood-building-new-college-scorecard-students; K. Sheehy, "3 Apps to Help High Schoolers Organize Their College Search," *USNWR*, January 6, 2014, retrieved from

http://www.usnews.com/education/blogs/high-school-notes/2014/01/06/3
-apps-to-help-high-schoolers-organize-their-college-search.

34. Bureau of Labor Statistics, "Employment Projections," *U.S. Department of Labor*, 2016, retrieved from https://www.bls.gov/emp/ep_chart_001.htm.

35. Hoxby and Avery, "Missing 'One-Offs.'"

36. There are differences in success in some majors and in the quality of the experience.

37. S. Goldrick-Rab, *Paying the Price: College Costs, Financial Aid, and the Betrayal of the American Dream* (Chicago: University of Chicago Press, 2016).

38. News articles about Chetty's work have focused on the relatively high incomes of students at selective colleges; again, the journalists who wrote these articles likely attended these schools. R. Chetty et al., "Mobility Report Cards"; D. Leonhardt, "America's Great Working-Class Colleges," *NYT*, January 18, 2017, retrieved from https://www.nytimes.com/2017/01/18/opinion/sunday/americas-great-working-class-colleges.html.

39. The highly selective privates should of course do what they can for low-income students, but given their class sizes, they can't make much of a dent in U.S. inequality.

40. https://www.questbridge.org/; http://ledascholars.org/; https://www.possefoundation.org/.

41. http://advisingcorps.org/.

42. S. Jaschik, "Is 'Undermatching' Overrated?," *IHE*, February 10, 2014, retrieved from https://www.insidehighered.com/news/2014/02/10/analysis-questions-assumptions-behind-undermatching-theory.

43. C. M. Steele, *Whistling Vivaldi: How Stereotypes Affect Us and What We Can Do* (New York: W. W. Norton, 2010).

44. In a detailed study of the sociology of low-income students at schools with high affluence, Elizabeth Armstrong and Laura Hamilton show in their book *Paying for the Party* that colocation of low-income students with affluent students has a number of negative consequences. Armstrong and Hamilton studied women in a so-called party dorm at a large midwestern university. In their study, most of the low-income students did not graduate or gravitated toward easy majors with low employment prospects. Affluent students in these same majors still had good outcomes because of the influence of their family wealth and status. E. A. Armstrong and L. T. Hamilton, *Paying for the Party: How College Maintains Inequality* (Cambridge, Mass.: Harvard University Press, 2013).

CHAPTER 5

1. JBL Associates and American Federation of Teachers, "Reversing Course: The Troubled State of Academic Staffing and a Path Forward," *American Federation of Teachers*, 2008, retrieved from http://files.eric.ed.gov/fulltext/ED503538.pdf.

2. R. Wilson, "Back in the Classroom," *CHE*, October 16, 2011, retrieved from http://www.chronicle.com/article/Colleges-Are-Calling/129429.

3. D. N. Figlio, M. O. Schapiro, and K. B. Soter, "Are Tenure Track Professors Better Teachers?," *National Bureau of Economic Research*, September 2013, retrieved from http://www.nber.org/papers/w19406.

4. http://www.wesleyan.edu/president/biography/courses.html.

5. G. Anders, "Good News Liberal-Arts Majors: Your Peers Probably Won't Outearn You Forever," *WSJ*, September 11, 2016, retrieved from https://www.wsj.com/articles/good-news-liberal-arts-majors-your-peers-probably-wont-outearn-you-forever-1473645902.

6. S. Dynarski, "Laptops Are Great, but Not during a Lecture or Meeting," *NYT*, November 22, 2017, retrieved from https://www.nytimes.com/2017/11/22/business/laptops-not-during-lecture-or-meeting.html.

7. Approximately one in four students at degree-granting postsecondary institutions were enrolled in a distance education course in fall 2014. National Center for Education Statistics, "Digest of Education Statistics," 2016, retrieved from https://nces.ed.gov/fastfacts/display.asp?id=80.

8. S. Eddy and K. A. Hogan, "Getting under the Hood: How and for Whom Does Increasing Course Structure Work?," *CBE–Life Sciences Education* 13, no. 3 (2014): 453–68; P. Tough, "Who Gets to Graduate?," *New York Times Magazine*, May 15, 2014, retrieved from https://www.nytimes.com/2014/05/18/magazine/who-gets-to-graduate.html.

9. General Assembly of the State of North-Carolina, *Act Establishing the University of North Carolina, 1789* (Laws of North-Carolina, 1789), 14–16, retrieved from http://docsouth.unc.edu/unc/unc01-08/unc01-08.html.

10. V. Larivière, Y. Gingras, and É. Archambault, "The Decline in the Concentration of Citations, 1900–2007," *Journal of the American Society for Information Science and Technology* 60, no. 4 (2009): 858–62.

11. S. Pearlstein, "Four Tough Things Universities Should Do to Rein in Costs," *WP*, November 25, 2015, retrieved from https://www.washingtonpost.com/opinions/four-tough-things-universities-should-do-to-rein-in-costs/2015/11/25/64fed3de-92c0-11e5-a2d6-f57908580b1f_story.html.

12. C. Flaherty, "So Much to Do, So Little Time," *IHE*, April 9, 2014, retrieved from https://www.insidehighered.com/news/2014/04/09/research-shows-professors-work-long-hours-and-spend-much-day-meetings; J. Fruscione, "When a College Contracts 'Adjunctivitis' It's the Students Who Lose," *PBS Newshour*, July 25, 2014, retrieved from http://www.pbs.org/newshour/making-sense/when-a-college-contracts-adjunctivitis-its-the-students-who-lose/.

13. Bran Ferren, "Lunch Keynote: Re-Imagining American Innovation at National Competitiveness Forum 2016" (video file), retrieved from https://www.youtube.com/watch?v=V_uzLNjNE7Q.

14. K. Davidson, *Carl Sagan: A Life* (New York: John Wiley and Sons, 1999).

15. The protection of compensation by tenure varies from state to state, depending on the attitude of the courts. Typically, the university has the ability to lower the salary of a tenured faculty member but not to zero.

16. A. Thomason, "Judges Award Back Pay to Chapel Hill Professor Imprisoned in Argentina," *CHE*, June 16, 2015, retrieved from http://www.chronicle.com/blogs/ticker/judges-award-back-pay-to-unc-professor-infamous-for-argentine-imprisonment/100759.

17. J. S. Cohen, "University of Illinois OKs $875,000 Settlement to End Steven Salaita Dispute," *Chicago Tribune*, November 12, 2015, retrieved from http://www.chicagotribune.com/news/local/breaking/ct-steven-salaita-settlement-met-20151112-story.html.

CHAPTER 6

1. American Association of University Professors Committee on College and University Governance, "College and University Governance: The University of Virginia's Governing Board's Attempt to Remove the President," 2013, retrieved from https://www.aaup.org/report/college-and-university-governance-university-virginia-governing-board%E2%80%99s-attempt-remove.

2. P. T. Jones II, "Op-Ed: Aspiring to Achieve Greatness," *Charlottesville Daily Progress*, June 17, 2012, retrieved from http://www.dailyprogress.com/news/op-ed-aspiring-to-achieve-greatness/article_be382c81-3059-56a2-81c5-3eb85627c978.html.

3. American Association of University Professors Committee on College and University Governance, "College and University Governance."

4. C. M. Hoxby, "The Economics of Online Postsecondary Education: MOOCs, Nonselective Education, and Highly Selective Education," *National Bureau of Economic Research*, 2014, retrieved from http://www.nber.org/papers/w19816.

5. A. B. Giamatti, *A Free and Ordered Space: The Real World of the University* (New York: W. W. Norton, 1988).

6. J. Stripling, "How Missouri's Deans Plotted to Get Rid of Their Chancellor," *CHE*, November 20, 2015, retrieved from http://www.chronicle.com/article/How-Missouri-s-Deans-Plotted/234283.

7. A. Finder, P. D. Healy, and K. Zernike, "President of Harvard Resigns, Ending Stormy 5-Year Tenure," *NYT*, February 22, 2006, retrieved from http://www.nytimes.com/2006/02/22/education/22harvard.html.

8. D. Shalala and A. Bernstein, "On Changing Academic Culture from the Inside: An Interview with Donna Shalala," *Change* 21, no. 1 (1989): 20–29, quotation at 20.

9. Michigan has the unique feature of having a board that is elected on public ballots in general elections.

10. D. Jesse and M. Snyder, "Michigan Athletic Director Dave Brandon Resigns," *USA Today*, October 31, 2014, retrieved from https://www.usatoday.com/story/sports/ncaaf/2014/10/31/michigan-athletic-director-dave-brandon/18236245/; S. Svrluga, "Mount St. Mary's University President Resigns," *WP*, February 29, 2016, retrieved from https://www.washingtonpost.com/news/grade-point/wp/2016/02/29/mount-st-marys-future-direction-on-the-table-as-leaders-meet-today/.

11. V. Luckerson, "College Divestment Movement Takes on Fossil Fuels after Battling Apartheid with Mandela," *Time*, December 10, 2013, retrieved from http://nation.time.com/2013/12/10/college-divestment-movement-takes-on-fossil-fuels-after-battling-apartheid-with-mandela/.

12. Ford Foundation, "For Foundation Commits $1 Billion from Endowment to Mission-Related Investments," April 5, 2017, retrieved from https://www.fordfoundation.org/the-latest/news/ford-foundation-commits-1-billion-from-endowment-to-mission-related-investments/.

13. M. Stratford, "Billion-Dollar Targets," *IHE*, February 16, 2016, retrieved from https://www.insidehighered.com/news/2016/02/16/congress-returns-scrutiny-wealthy-university-endowments.

14. R. Brooks, "Renaming University Buildings with Racist Namesakes Is an Uphill Battle," *USA Today*, February 14, 2017, retrieved from http://college.usatoday.com/2017/02/14/renaming-university-buildings-with-racist-namesakes-is-an-uphill-battle/; M. B. Marklein, "College Hopefuls Look for Green Universities," *USA Today*, September 16, 2011, retrieved from https://usatoday30.usatoday.com/news/education/2011-04-20-green-college-campus-princeton-review.htm#mainstory.

15. "But for Ohio State Campaign Tops $3 Billion," *Ohio State University*, September 29, 2016, retrieved from https://news.osu.edu/news/2016/09/29/but-for-ohio-state-campaign-tops-3-billion/; E. Pyle, "OSU Wants $100 Million for In-State Scholarships," *Columbus Dispatch*, February 1, 2013, retrieved from http://www.dispatch.com/content/stories/local/2013/02/01/ohio-state-wants-100-million-for-in-state-scholarships.html; E. Powers, "Life after the A.D. (Athletics Director)," *IHE*, July 10, 2006, retrieved from https://www.insidehighered.com/news/2006/07/10/vanderbilt; WDTV, "WVU's Devotion to Education a Focus of President Gee's Annual Fall Address," October 10, 2016, retrieved from http://www.wdtv.com/content/news/President-Gee-gives-annual-fall-address-396563841.html.

16. "The 20 Most Interesting College Presidents," *The Best Schools*, 2010, retrieved from http://www.thebestschools.org/features/most-interesting-college-presidents/.

17. E. G. Gee, "The President and the Board: Remarks at Southern University Conference," *West Virginia University*, April 9, 2016, retrieved from http://presidentgee.wvu.edu/speeches/the-president-and-the-board.

CHAPTER 7

1. E. Ehrlich, "NIH's Role in Sustaining the U.S. Economy 2016 Update," *United for Medical Research*, 2016, retrieved from http://www.unitedformedicalresearch .com/advocacy_reports/nihs-role-in-sustaining-the-us-economy-2/.

2. "Teaching Hospitals: Vital for Tomorrow's Health Care," *American Hospital Association*, 2013, retrieved from https://www.aha.org/infographics/ 2013-12-11-teaching-hospitals-vital-tomorrows-health-care.

3. E. J. Heisler et al., "Federal Support for Graduate Medical Education: An Overview," *Congressional Research Service*, February 12, 2016, retrieved from https://fas.org/sgp/crs/misc/R44376.pdf.

4. In 1994, Brigham and Women's Hospital and Massachusetts General Hospital, two renowned medical centers, founded Partners HealthCare. The Partners member and collaboration network consists of more than forty hospitals, community health centers, and health programs, several of which are affiliated with Harvard Medical School and employ several members of the medical school faculty. Partners is renowned for its biomedical research and innovative health services. Physicians at Brigham and Women's Hospital performed the first triple-organ transplant in the United States in 1995, and in 1981 researchers at Massachusetts General contributed to the development of the first artificial skin made from living cells. Today, the Partners HealthCare system operates throughout the nation, as well as globally under the subsidiary Partners HealthCare International. Harvard Medical School, "HMS Affiliates," *Harvard Medical School*, 2017, retrieved from https://hms.harvard.edu/about -hms/hms-affiliates; Partners HealthCare, "About Partners Healthcare," 2017, retrieved from http://www.partners.org/About/Default.aspx.

5. Barnes-Jewish Hospital, St. Louis Children's Hospital, and the Washington University in St. Louis School of Medicine are all colocated on the Washington University Medical Campus, which spans over seventeen city blocks. Together, these medical centers help to drive economic development in St. Louis through contributing approximately four billion dollars annually to the metropolitan region and employing more than twenty thousand people. BJC HealthCare is nationally recognized for thoracic surgery, orthopedics, cancer treatment, and pediatric care. Barnes-Jewish Hospital, "History," 2017, retrieved from http://www.barnesjewish.org/About-Us/History; St. Louis Children's Hospital, "About Us," 2017, retrieved from http://www.stlouischildrens.org/about-us; Washington University School of Medicine in St. Louis, "Washington University Medical Campus," 2017, retrieved from https://medicine.wustl.edu/about/ medical-center/.

6. The University of Pittsburgh Medical Center (UPMC) is an organization of more than twenty-five hospitals that generates almost $900 million yearly and employs more than sixty-five thousand people. UPMC is affiliated with

the University of Pittsburgh Schools of the Health Sciences, and together they are international leaders in transplantation, cancer treatment, neurosurgery, psychiatry, orthopedics, and sports medicine. University of Pittsburgh Medical Center, "Why UPMC?," 2017, retrieved from http://www.upmc.com/about/why-upmc/pages/default.aspx.

7. Missouri Economic Research and Information Center, "Missouri's Top 50 Employers," *Missouri Department of Economic Development,* 2016, retrieved from https://www.missourieconomy.org/industry/top50/index.stm; University of Pittsburgh Medical Center, "Why UPMC?"

8. As an example, although Lehigh University doesn't have a medical school, it has adroitly made health-related education part of its strategic plan. N. Anderson, "Lehigh Aims to Expand 20 Percent, Add Health College," January 6, 2017, retrieved from https://www.washingtonpost.com/news/grade-point/wp/2017/01/06/lehigh-aims-to-expand-20-percent-add-health-college/.

9. K. A. Holbrook and P. R. Sanberg, "Understanding the High Cost of Success in University Research," *Technology and Innovation* 15, no. 3 (2013): 269–80.

10. Association of American Medical Colleges, "Academic Medicine Investment in Medical Research," 2015, retrieved from https://www.aamc.org/initiatives/research/.

11. C. Newfield, *The Great Mistake: How We Wrecked Public Universities and How We Can Fix Them* (Baltimore: Johns Hopkins University Press, 2016).

12. For more detail on the economics of academic medicine, see H. R. Bourne and E. B. Vermillion, *Follow the Money: Funding Research in a Large Academic Health Center* (San Francisco: University of California Medical Humanities Press, 2016).

13. W. A. Link, *William Friday: Power, Purpose, and American Higher Education* (Chapel Hill: University of North Carolina Press, 1995).

14. H. Meisel, "A Closer Look at What Led to the U of I Chancellor's Resignation," *Northern Public Radio,* August 19, 2015, retrieved from http://northernpublicradio.org/post/closer-look-what-led-u-i-chancellors-resignation.

15. R. Florida, *The Rise of the Creative Class Revisited: Revised and Expanded* (New York, N.Y.: Basic Books, 2011).

16. J. Pope, "Could a Private University Have Made a Difference in Detroit?," *Atlantic,* July 27, 2013, retrieved from https://www.theatlantic.com/national/archive/2013/07/could-a-private-university-have-made-a-difference-in-detroit/278148/.

17. J. J. Duderstadt, *The View from the Helm: Leading the American University during an Era of Change* (Ann Arbor: University of Michigan Press, 2007), 119.

18. Newfield, *Great Mistake.*

19. National Science Foundation, "Ranking by Total R&D Expenditures," 2015, retrieved from https://ncsesdata.nsf.gov/profiles/site?method= rankingBySource&ds=herd; National Science Foundation, "University of Michigan, Ann Arbor Data," 2015, retrieved from https://ncsesdata.nsf.gov/ profiles/site?method=report&fice=2325&id=h2; National Science Foundation, "University of Washington, Seattle Data," retrieved from https://ncsesdata.nsf .gov/profiles/site?method=report&fice=330006&id=h2; National Science Foundation, "The University of North Carolina at Chapel Hill Data," 2015, retrieved from https://ncsesdata.nsf.gov/profiles/site?method=report&fice= 2974&id=h2.

20. V. Bush, *Science: The Endless Frontier*, 1945, retrieved from https://www .nsf.gov/od/lpa/nsf50/vbush1945.htm.

CHAPTER 8

1. M. Porter, "Colleges and Universities and Regional Economic Development: A Strategic Perspective," *Aspen Symposium, Forum for the Future of Higher Education*, 2006, retrieved from http://www.hbs.edu/faculty/ Pages/item.aspx?num=46840.

2. National Center for Education Statistics, "Digest of Education Statistics," 2016, retrieved from https://nces.ed.gov/fastfacts/display.asp?id=84; S. A. Ginder, J. E. Kelly-Reid, and F. B. Mann, "Enrollment and Employees in Postsecondary Institutions, Fall 2014; and Financial Statistics and Academic Libraries, Fiscal Year 2014," *National Center for Education Statistics*, November 2015, retrieved from https://nces.ed.gov/pubs2016/2016005.pdf; T. D. Snyder, ed., "120 Years of American Education: A Statistical Portrait," *National Center for Education Statistics*, January 1993, retrieved from https://nces.ed.gov/pubs93/93442.pdf.

3. In constant 2014–15 dollars; National Center for Education Statistics, "Postsecondary Institution Expenses," last updated May 2017, retrieved from https://nces.ed.gov/programs/coe/indicator_cue.asp.

4. Massachusetts Institute of Technology, "MIT Facts 2017: Entrepreneurship and Innovation," 2017, retrieved from http://web.mit.edu/ facts/entrepreneurship.html.

5. C. Pazzanese, "Harvard's Alumni Impact," *Harvard Gazette*, December 8, 2015, retrieved from http://news.harvard.edu/gazette/story/2015/12/ harvards-alumni-impact/.

6. J. Beckett, "Study Shows Stanford Alumni Create nearly $3 Trillion in Economic Impact Each Year," *Stanford News*, October 24, 2012, retrieved from http://news.stanford.edu/news/2012/october/innovation-economic -impact-102412.html.

7. University of North Carolina–Chapel Hill, "Analysis Finds UNC–Chapel Hill and UNC Health Care Medical Center Contribute over $7 Billion to North

Carolina Economy," *UNC News Archive*, February 18, 2015, retrieved from http://uncnewsarchive.unc.edu/2015/02/18/analysis-finds-unc-chapel -hill-unc-health-care-medical-center-contribute-7-billion-north-carolina -economy/; Economic Modeling Specialists International and Duke University, "Fact Sheet: Demonstrating the Economic Value of Duke University," *Duke University*, 2015, retrieved from https://today.duke.edu/showcase/mmedia/ pdf/duke-economic-value-fact-sheet-fy1213.pdf; North Carolina State University, "Think and Do," *North Carolina State University*, 2017, retrieved from https://www.ncsu.edu/think-and-do/research-realized/.

8. P. Basken, "Seeking Hip Worker Environs, Universities Remake Research Parks," *CHE*, October 21, 2014, retrieved from http://www.chronicle.com/ article/Seeking-Hip-Worker-Environs/149541/.

9. Boston Redevelopment Authority, "Boston by the Numbers: College and Universities," 2011, retrieved from http://www.bostonplans.org/ getattachment/3488e768-1dd4-4446-a557-3892bb0445c6/.

10. D. W. Chen, "Where Halls of Ivy Meet Silicon Dreams, a New City Rises," *NYT*, March 22, 2017, retrieved from https://www.nytimes.com/2017/03/22/ nyregion/nyc-cornell-columbia-nyu-campuses.html.

11. J. E. Lane, "Higher Education and Economic Competitiveness," in *Universities and Colleges as Economic Drivers: Measuring Higher Education's Role in Economic Development*, ed. J. E. Lane and D. B. Johnstone (Albany: SUNY Press, 2012).

12. B. Davis, "The Great Unraveling: There's an Antidote to America's Long Economic Malaise: College Towns," *WSJ*, December 12, 2016, retrieved from https://www.wsj.com/articles/theres-an-antidote-to-americas-long -economic-malaise-college-towns-1481558522.

13. Ibid.

14. Ibid.

15. Ibid.

16. Ibid.

17. A. Valero and J. Van Reenen, "How Universities Boost Economic Growth," *VOX, Center for Economic Policy and Research*, November 10, 2016, retrieved from http://voxeu.org/article/how-universities-boost-economic-growth.

18. S. J. Carroll and E. Erkut, "The Benefits to Taxpayers from Increases in Students' Educational Attainments," *Rand Corporation*, 2009, retrieved from http://www.rand.org/pubs/monographs/MG686.html.

19. J. Wiens and C. Jackson, "The Importance of Young Firms for Economic Growth," *Ewing Marion Kauffman Foundation*, September 13, 2015, retrieved from http://www.kauffman.org/what-we-do/resources/entrepreneurship -policy-digest/the-importance-of-young-firms-for-economic-growth.

20. Ibid.

21. Ibid.

22. Ibid.

23. Porter, "Colleges and Universities and Regional Economic Development."

24. L. Pappano, "Got the Next Great Idea?," *NYT*, July 19, 2012, retrieved from http://www.nytimes.com/2012/07/20/education/edlife/campus-incubators -are-on-the-rise-as-colleges-encourage-student-start-ups.html.

25. G. Blumenstyk, "Inventors, Hop aboard the Carolina Express (License)," *CHE*, December 9, 2009, retrieved from http://www.chronicle.com/article/ Inventors-Hop-Aboard-the/49450/.

26. L. Schoppe, "Ready-to-Sign Licensing Agreements: Does One Size Fit All?," *Fuentek*, March 7, 2011, retrieved from http://www.fuentek.com/ blog/2011/03/how-to-do-ready-to-sign-licensing/.

27. For an extensive discussion of this model, see our description of the Langer Lab at MIT in H. Thorp and B. Goldstein, *Engines of Innovation: The Entrepreneurial University in the Twenty-First Century* (Chapel Hill: University of North Carolina Press, 2010).

28. Ibid., 27–30.

29. See our discussion of DeSimone labs in ibid.

30. Deshpande Center for Technological Innovation, "Our Impact," *MIT*, 2017, retrieved from http://deshpande.mit.edu/about/our-impact.

31. S. Blank, "Why the Lean Start-Up Changes Everything," *Harvard Business Review*, May 2013, retrieved from https://hbr.org/2013/05/why-the-lean-start -up-changes-everything.

32. Ibid.

33. S. Blank, "Getting Out of the Building . . . By Staying in the Building!," December 30, 2014, retrieved from https://steveblank.com/2014/12/.

34. National Science Foundation, "NSF Fosters Entrepreneurship, Innovation through New Awards for I-Corps Nodes," September 27, 2016, retrieved from https://www.nsf.gov/news/news_summ.jsp?cntn_id=189600.

35. The State Science and Technology Institute, "Universities Re-Imagine Alumni Engagement with Angel Networks, Crowdfunding," November 13, 2014, retrieved from http://ssti.org/blog/universities-re-imagine-alumni -engagement-angel-networks-crowdfunding.

36. B. Tedeschi, "The Idea Incubator Goes to Campus," *NYT*, June 26, 2010, retrieved from http://www.nytimes.com/2010/06/27/business/27incubate .html.

37. D. Ranii, "Duke University, Alumni Eye Investments in Startups," *News and Observer*, March 11, 2015, retrieved from http://www.newsobserver.com/ news/business/article13451312.html.

38. The authors each have a financial interest in Hatteras Venture Partners.

39. M. A. Reslinski and B. S. Wu, "The Value of Royalty," *Nature Biotechnology* 34 (2016): 685–90.

40. For a full discussion of how collaboration with nonacademic entities improves academic science and an effective tech transfer mechanism retains faculty, see chapters 2 and 7 in *Engines of Innovation*. St. Louis has bucked this trend with the Cortex Innovation District, where a diversified group of tenants—not just university-based startups—have fueled the rebirth of an important section of the city.

41. A. D. Higginson and M. R. Munafò, "Current Incentives for Scientists Lead to Underpowered Studies with Erroneous Conclusions," *PLOS Biology* 14, no. 11 (2016): 1–14.

CHAPTER 9

1. S. Mukherjee, "IBM Workers to Use Watson Supercomputer to Find Cancer Treatments," *Fortune*, October 11, 2016, retrieved from http://fortune .com/2016/10/11/ibm-watson-empoyees-cancer-drugs/.

2. J. Lorin, "The Pill That Made Northwestern Rich," *Bloomberg*, August 18, 2016, retrieved from https://www.bloomberg.com/news/articles/2016-08-18/ the-pill-that-made-northwestern-rich.

3. European Commission, "Entrepreneurship in Education," 2017, retrieved from http://ec.europa.eu/education/policy/strategic-framework/ entrepreneurship_en.

4. J. K. H. Mok and K. Yue, "Promoting Entrepreneurship and Innovation in China: Transformations in University Curriculum and Research Capacity," in *Higher Education in the BRICS Countries: Investigating the Pact between Higher Education and Society*, ed. S. Schwartzman, R. Pinheiro, and P. Pillay (Dordrecht, Netherlands: Springer, 2015).

5. P. F. Drucker, *Innovation and Entrepreneurship* (New York: HarperCollins, 1985), viii.

6. That is how we two formed our partnership.

CHAPTER 10

1. D. Hall, "A College Education Isn't Just about Job Prospects," *Hechinger Report*, July 12, 2013, retrieved from http://hechingerreport.org/a-college -education-isnt-just-about-job-prospects/.

2. C. Rampell, "Why Do Americans Go to College? First and Foremost, They Want Better Jobs," *WP*, February 17, 2015, retrieved from https://www .washingtonpost.com/news/rampage/wp/2015/02/17/why-do-americans -go-to-college-first-and-foremost-they-want-better-jobs/.

3. J. G. Altonji and S. D. Zimmerman, "The Costs of and Net Returns to College Major," *National Bureau of Economic Research*, January 2017, retrieved from http://www.nber.org/papers/w23029.

4. S. M. Butler, "Business Is Likely to Reshape Higher Ed," *Brookings Institution*, December 20, 2016, retrieved from https://www.brookings.edu/opinions/business-is-likely-to-reshape-higher-ed/.

5. T. S. Bernard, "A Brighter Job Market, for Some," *NYT*, April 8, 2016, retrieved from https://www.nytimes.com/2016/04/10/education/edlife/a-brighter-job-market-for-some.html.

6. S. Dominus, "How to Get a Job with a Philosophy Degree," *NYT*, September 13, 2013, retrieved from http://www.nytimes.com/2013/09/15/magazine/how-to-get-a-job-with-a-philosophy-degree.html.

7. D. J. Deming, C. Goldin, and L. F. Katz, "The For-Profit Postsecondary School Sector: Nimble Critters or Agile Predators?," *National Bureau of Economic Research*, December 2011, retrieved from http://www.nber.org/papers/w17710.

8. Bernard, "Brighter Job Market."

9. A. Chan, "Stop Asking How Much Your Major Will Pay Off after Graduation," *LinkedIn*, May 11, 2015, retrieved from https://www.linkedin.com/pulse/education-beyond-majors-jobs-earnings-andy-chan.

10. National Association of Colleges and Employers, "Job Outlook 2016: The Attributes Employers Want to See on New College Graduates' Resumes," *National Association of Colleges and Employers*, 2016, retrieved from https://www.naceweb.org/career-development/trends-and-predictions/job-outlook-2016-attributes-employers-want-to-see-on-new-college-graduates-resumes/.

11. Ibid.

12. J. Wind and D. Reibstein, "Reinventing Training for the Global Information Age," *Wharton School of University of Pennsylvania*, August 30, 2000, retrieved from https://faculty.wharton.upenn.edu/wp-content/uploads/2012/04/0011_Reinventing_Training_for_the_Global.pdf.

13. J. Gonzalez, "Project Based Learning: Start Here," *Cult of Pedagogy*, June 26, 2016, retrieved from https://www.cultofpedagogy.com/project-based-learning/.

14. Gallup, Inc., "Great Jobs, Great Lives: The 2014 Gallup-Purdue Index Report," 2014, retrieved from https://www.luminafoundation.org/files/resources/galluppurdueindex-report-2014.pdf.

15. Altonji and Zimmerman, "Costs of and Net Returns to College Major."

16. Some schools stress average starting salary as an important metric, but there are strong reasons to reject this measure because of its short-term time horizon and its bias toward certain high-paying professions.

17. H. Thorp and B. Goldstein, *Engines of Innovation: The Entrepreneurial University in the Twenty-First Century* (Chapel Hill: University of North Carolina Press, 2010).

18. The accreditation process can often be a major impediment to the involvement of nontraditional faculty and must be addressed if universities

are to truly open the tent to nonacademics. Typically, accreditation agencies require all faculty to have at least an undergraduate degree, and full members of the faculty are required to have a terminal degree, typically a doctorate. Nontraditional faculty usually do not have a Ph.D., and in some cases they don't have a college degree at all. One of our favorite colleagues is a brilliant teacher of artistic entrepreneurship. He managed Crosby, Stills, and Nash for many years and then built a distinguished career in the music business, but he never graduated from college. After years of teaching and mentoring students, accreditation requirements prohibit him from being listed as the professor of record. This is a particular problem in the arts and writing programs, where real-world experience does not always come along with a bachelor's degree. For those who have graduated from college but do not have a terminal degree, a number of positions are emerging, including professor of the practice, artist in residence, and entrepreneur in residence. These titles confer faulty status but also meet accreditation demands.

19. M. Stein, pers. comm., July 11, 2017.

20. Brown University, "BrownConnect," 2017, retrieved from https://brownconnect.brown.edu/.

21. S. Dominus, "How to Get a Job with a Philosophy Degree," *NYT*, September 13, 2013, retrieved from http://www.nytimes.com/2013/09/15/magazine/how-to-get-a-job-with-a-philosophy-degree.html.

22. Ibid.

23. Ibid.

24. Ibid.

25. Ibid.

26. The Education Trust, "College Results Online," 2017, retrieved from http://www.collegeresults.org/default.aspx.

27. K. Kiley, "Another Liberal Arts Critic," *IHE*, January 30, 2013, retrieved from https://www.insidehighered.com/news/2013/01/30/north-carolina -governor-joins-chorus-republicans-critical-liberal-arts.

CHAPTER 11

1. N. Savidge, "New Regents President Calls for UW to Recruit Chancellors from Private Sector," *Wisconsin State Journal*, July 8, 2017, retrieved from http://host.madison.com/wsj/news/local/education/university/new-regents -president-calls-for-uw-to-recruit-chancellors-from/article_b05a9b95-f3c2 -5689-9138-8f3cf3b4cce2.html.

2. Pew Research Center, "Sharp Partisan Divisions in Views of National Institutions," 2017, retrieved from http://assets.pewresearch.org/wp-content/uploads/sites/5/2017/07/11101505/07-10-17-Institutions-release.pdf.

3. Gallup, Inc., "Great Jobs, Great Lives: The 2014 Gallup-Purdue Index Report," 2014, retrieved from https://www.luminafoundation.org/files/resources/galluppurdueindex-report-2014.pdf.

CHAPTER 12

1. At public universities, where a majority of college students are educated, governors and state legislators often appoint trustees, and in some states they are elected. We thus grouped trustees and policymakers together.

2. Nonacademics, often politicians, have successfully run university systems, but that job typically involves allocation of resources and negotiating with government officials, which is a fundamentally different task from building and maintaining a learning community.

Index

AAMC (Association of American Medical Colleges), 94

academia, 7, 21, 38, 67–68, 75, 81, 119, 125, 148; attractions of, 110; business and, 14, 32, 34, 117; commercialization and, 114; economic impact of, 106; innovation and entrepreneurship and, 111, 116; private sector and, 63, 120–23; public and, 98, 119

academic freedom, 5, 66; faculty and, 17, 60, 108; governance and, 15–16; tenure and, 68, 70

academic journals, 66–67

academic medicine: as elephant in the room, 89–97; as huge economic engine, 95–96; presidents and, 144. *See also* medical centers, academic; medical schools

accessibility, 67, 88; importance of, 52–53; threats to, 54–55

accountability, 5, 17

accreditation, 2, 173–74n18

ACT, 57

Adams, John, 48

Adams, John Quincy, 48

adjunct faculty, 61, 62, 67, 133, 146

administration, administrators, 7, 16, 30, 73, 75, 135, 142; building learning community, 59; faculty and, 17, 61; rebuilding partnership between public and universities and, 143–45; research and, 66, 146; teaching and, 62, 146; tenure and, 69, 71

admissions, 50; big data approach in, 29–30; policies and standards of, 2, 24, 49

advising, academic, 148

affirmative action, 57

affordability of higher education, 15, 19, 55, 132, 138. *See also* accessibility; tuition

African Americans, 20, 23, 57. *See also* blacks; HBCUs; people of color

all-female education, 36, 43, 46

all-male education, 37

alma mater, 8

alt-acs, 61

alumni, 17, 27, 37, 38, 43, 73, 81, 99, 105, 114; discontent of, 33, 40; identity and loyalty of, 5, 8, 34, 42; internships and, 128; magazines of, 39; vision creation and, 41–42

American colleges and universities: challenges of, 18–32, 141; closures of, 20, 33, 38, 43; evolution of, 14; financial ("arithmetic") problems of, 21–24, 46, 86; models for, 15; origins of, 52; problems facing, 20–27; superiority of, 3, 9; threats to, 19–20. *See also* elite colleges and universities

American Dream, 49, 50, 56

American economy, 4, 7, 98, 108, 133. *See also* economic development; Great Recession

American higher education: liberal arts and sciences in, 9–11; strengths of, 7; superiority of, 82, 143; traditional model of, 4, 25, 27; uniqueness of, 118

American higher education, trends in, 7–8, 24, 129; as promising opportunities, 28–32

East Carolina School of Medicine, 96
Eastern Michigan University, 9–10
economic development, 135, 167n5;
    importance of, 98–108
economic impact, maximizing, 101–8
Economic Policy Institute, 51
economics, economists, 10, 55–56,
    65, 132
economies of scale, 28
Education Trust, 129
EdX, 25
efficiency, efficiencies, 24, 30, 34, 40, 65,
    75; of cost, 68, 70
Einstein, Albert, 10
elite colleges and universities, 6, 24,
    35, 48, 54, 55, 72; affordability of and
    financial aid at, 19, 22. *See also* private
    colleges and universities; selective
    colleges and universities
Emory University, 97
employees, 7; faculty not as, 60–71; non-
    tenured faculty as, 62; professional, 30
employers, skills sought by, 122–23
employment: preparation for, 4, 7, 10, 47,
    63, 119, 134; rates of, 4, 51; at universi-
    ties, 98
endowments, 6, 15, 22, 24, 31, 43, 79; for
    specific programs or objectives, 105,
    146
engagement, 144, 146, 147; faculty, 66–68;
    with students, 67, 138; within work-
    place, 123, 133
engineering, 52, 58, 121
engines of economic growth, universi-
    ties as, 98, 108, 133
Engines of Innovation (Thorp and
    Goldstein, 2010), 1, 108, 109, 129, 153n1
enrollments, dropping, 2, 43, 131
entrepreneurialism and entrepre-
    neurship, 46, 99, 105, 135, 174n18;
    basic research vs., 109–18; entrepre-
    neurs-in-residence and, 117, 118; as

reality, 115–18; teaching of, 62, 113–14;
    universities and, 1, 102
ethnicity and race, 20, 23, 50, 57. *See also*
    African Americans; Asian Americans;
    blacks; diversity; Latinx
European Union, 115
expectations, 95, 119, 137; for economic
    development, 106–7; of faculty, 47–48,
    60, 67; of public, 7, 31, 95, 98, 99, 135; of
    students and parents, 47, 59, 113, 120,
    124, 134, 147
expenses, 21, 23–24, 40
experiential learning, 30, 65, 118, 127–28;
    workplace engagement and, 123–24.
    See also internships
expertise, experts, 15, 37, 105, 123, 137
extracurricular activities, 124, 147

faculty, 7, 8, 37, 40, 43, 45, 73, 75, 84, 91,
    116, 118, 120, 133; academic freedom
    and, 17, 108; elitism of, 137; engage-
    ment of, 66–68, 145–46; expectations
    of, 16–17; field recruitment by, 10–11;
    governance and, 15–16, 17, 39, 42, 73,
    132, 138; as leaders and administra-
    tors, 61, 144; in learning communities,
    59, 123; as nonemployees, 60–71;
    part-time, 61, 67, 145; peer review and,
    15, 69, 132; in rebuilding partnership
    between public and universities
    and, 145–46; research and, 12–14,
    110, 114; retirement of, 69; retraining
    of, 105, 126; reward system for, 126,
    136, 138, 145; salaries of, 23–24, 135,
    165n15; self-conception of, 47–48; as
    technology averse, 26; trustees and,
    81–82; types of, 61, 133, 145, 173–74n18;
    visibility of, 145–46. *See also* academic
    freedom; adjunct faculty; deans;
    governance, university; tenure
Faculty Boot Camp on entrepreneurship
    (UNC), 105

faculty practice plan, 92

faculty-to-student ratio, 28

Farmer, Steve, 11, 20

federal government: higher education and, 5, 37, 53, 77, 93; research funded by, 12, 13, 14, 23, 89, 93–94, 107, 114, 132. *See also* Morrill Act; Pell Grants; U.S. Congress; U.S. Department of Education

feminist movement, 36

Ferren, Bran, 67

financial aid, 7, 53, 54, 57, 79; at elite schools, 22, 41, 55, 157n30. *See also* Pell Grants

financial problems of universities, 6, 21–24, 39, 72

Financing American Higher Education in the Era of Globalization (Zumeta et al., 2012), 21

fixed-term faculty, 61

flipped classrooms, 29, 30, 130

Folt, Carol, 41, 77, 80, 120, 137, 139

Ford Foundation, 79

foreign language requirements, 143

foreign students, 6, 23, 24

for-profit higher education industry, 2, 21, 28, 55, 59; failings of, 51–52; metrics of, 121, 124

foundations, 85, 93, 94. *See also names of individual foundations*

Frampton, Paul, 69

freedom of expression on campus, 16

Friday, William, 96

Friga, Paul, 36

Full Sail University, 52

fundraising, 16, 80, 82, 145; Wrighton and, 82, 85. *See also* donations, donors

funds flow, medical schools and, 92–93

Gallup-Purdue index, 123–24, 126, 127, 129; on mentors, 138–39

Gates, Bill, 48

Gates Foundation, 94

Gee, Gordon, 63, 78, 85, 138; on compact, 50, 88; as university leader, 82–84; on university leaders, 80, 83–84, 87–88

general education courses, 10

genomics, 95

George Mason University, 35

Germany, 15

Giamatti, Bart, 5, 76; on university presidents, 6, 74–75

GI Bill (1944), 14, 49, 53; for-profit universities and, 51, 52

globalization, 20, 40, 167n4

goal setting, 129, 147–48

Goldstein, Buck, 62, 105, 171n38

Good to Great (Collins, 2001), 33

goodwill, 96, 144

Google, 19, 122

governance, university, 4, 42, 71, 78, 82; complex structure of, 76–77; faculty and, 15–16, 17, 34, 39, 42, 60, 61, 68, 73, 132, 138

governors, state, 73, 76, 132–36, 175n1

graduate education, 36, 143, 145, 146

graduate students, 15, 55, 81, 93, 146; challenges of, 148–49; research and, 13, 115; teaching by, 61, 62, 133, 145

graduation rates, 29, 52, 56; at elite schools, 54, 58

grants, ignition, 105, 106

Grassley, Charles, 22

Great American University, The (Cole, 2009), 12

Great Mistake, The (Newfield, 2016), 94

Great Recession of 2008, 22, 40, 45, 100, 101; effects of, 23, 54, 63, 136

Hamilton (musical; Miranda), 48

Hamilton, Alexander, 48

Hamilton, Laura, 163n44

science, 12, 37, 84, 90, 95, 104, 109,
113. *See also* biomedical research;
engineering; research; technology
Science (journal), 114
Science: The Endless Frontier (V. Bush,
1945), 12
selective colleges and universities,
163n38; low-income students and,
56–57, 58, 163n39. *See also* elite
colleges and universities; private
colleges universities
Selingo, Jeff, 21, 26, 45, 52, 119
semester-long projects, 123, 124
seminars, 29, 146
Shakespeare, William, 10
Shalala, Donna, 75, 76
Shanahan, Suzanne, 38
Silicon Valley, 105
silos in universities, 116
Simon, John, 72–73
skepticism over higher education, 3
social media, 25, 122, 138
social mobility, 4, 6, 14–15, 17, 21, 50
soft skills, 122, 123
Southern University Conference
(2016), 83
Spellings, Margaret, 18, 76
Spelman College, 36
staff, value of, 138–39
Stanford University, 29, 45, 56, 57, 99,
101, 113
start-ups, 101, 103, 105, 114
Starving the Beast (2016 documentary), 30
state support: conditions for, 133; of
public universities, 22, 23, 27, 52–53,
54, 74
state university systems, 76, 77
St. Catharine College, closure of, 20, 44
STEM (science, technology, engineering, and math) fields, 37
stipends, 127–28
St. Louis, 96, 99, 167n5, 172n40

St. Louis Children's Hospital, 167n5
strategy and strategic planning, 37, 80,
102, 168n8; difficulty of, 36–38; importance of, 33–36; at Sweet Briar, 43–44
Strayer University, 51
Struggle to Reform Our Colleges, The
(Bok, 2017), 28
student amenities, 59
student centers, 118
student government, 132
student loans and debt, 6, 19, 51, 54;
consequences of, 55–56; default rates
of, 55–56; level of, 14, 18, 55, 56, 121
students, 4, 7, 21, 24, 27, 31, 49, 91, 134, 147;
choice of course of study by, 10–11;
college leadership and, 143–44; concerns of, 119–20, 133; engagement of,
123, 133, 147; expectations of, 59, 119,
134; faculty engagement with, 67; his-
torical relationship with, 50–52; listening to, 137–38; narratives about, 47–48,
49; as non-customers, 47–59, 135;
nontraditional, 128, 148; in rebuilding partnership between public and
universities, 147–49; relationship of, to
university, 27–28; support University
of Virginia president, 73, 75; welcoming of, 139–40. *See also* graduate
students; undergraduate students
substance abuse, 138
Sullivan, Teresa, 71, 72–74, 75
Summers, Larry, 75
surveys and polls, 3, 18–19, 39
Swan Lake, 67–68
Sweet Briar College, 87; closure of, 27,
33; crisis response at, 43–44

taxpayers, 135–36
tax reform, 131
tax revenues, 101, 107, 135
teaching, 21, 25, 30, 126; by administrators, 62, 144; of entrepreneurial

thinking, 113–14, 116; as essential faculty responsibility, 60–62, 145, 146; by lectures, 25, 64–65, 123, 126; online, 26, 29, 65, 72, 81; research and, 135, 137, 146; students and, 133, 145; successful, 63–65. *See also* faculty; learning; MOOCs; pedagogy; technology

teaching hospitals, 90, 91–93, 144. *See also* academic medicine; medical centers, academic; medical schools

technology, 74, 95, 100, 101, 122, 136; as opportunity, 28, 29–30, 52, 65, 103; as problem, 24–27, 46, 86. *See also* inventions and patents; MOOCs; online education

technology transfer, 106, 109, 114; offices of, 13–14, 92, 103, 107

TED Talks, 25, 65

tenure, 5, 15, 42, 60, 138, 145; cost-effectiveness of, 6, 70, 133; essential need for, 68–71; protections of, 131, 165n15

tenure-track faculty, 146, 148–49

term limits of trustees, 79

Texas, 20

Thorp, Holden, 62, 75, 87, 105, 171n38

3M, 96

Thrun, Sebastian, 29

Toward a More Perfect University (Cole, 2016), 3, 12

tradition, importance of, 42

traditional students, 28, 148

transactional relationship between students and universities, 4, 47, 50, 55, 59, 129, 135

translational medicine, 95, 109

transparency about credential of college degree, 124–25

Tressel, Jim, 83

trustees, 5, 43, 69, 73, 76, 89, 97, 108, 119, 137; chair of, 132, 134, 135; complicated

role of, 77–82; faculty and, 81–82; presidents and, 80, 84; of public universities, 78, 165n9, 175n11; in rebuilding partnership between public and universities and, 141–43; selection of, 78–79, 165n9; undergraduate education and, 81, 87, 90, 143; of UNC, Chapel Hill, 34, 111; of University of Virginia, 71, 72–74

tuition, 7, 43, 54; discounts in rates, 22; inflation rate outpaced by tuition increases, 22; policy concerning, 56, 74; rising cost of, 14, 18, 21, 22, 45, 54, 59, 136

Udacity, 25, 29

underemployment, 121

undergraduate education, 51, 81, 87, 90, 143, 145; demand for, 20, 51, 55

undergraduate students, 58, 113; extra-curricular activities and, 147; idealism of, 137; research by, 30, 127, 147; student debt of, 55; teaching of, 61, 62; universities and, 47–59, 160n2. *See also* students

undermatching, 56–57

unionization of adjunct faculty, 62, 146

United Kingdom, 3, 13, 15

United Negro College Fund, 15, 36, 50, 120

Universities. *See* colleges and universities

university, the, 8, 15, 47, 99; purpose of, 99

"university effect," 101

University of Arizona, Tucson, 44

University of Bologna, 15

University of California, Berkeley, 23

University of California, San Diego, 103

University of California, Santa Barbara, 17, 36

University of California System, 38, 162n28